HONORING
THE LEGACY

HONORING THE LEGACY

A Guide of African-American Monuments and Statues

Tammy Gibson

Written By: Tammy Gibson © 2020

Published By: Pen Legacy®

Cover By: Christian Cuan

Edited By: Abigail Summer

Photo By: Claudia Parker Portraits & Productions

DISCLAIMER. The statues and monuments listed were at all locations at the time of publishing. However, due to the racial tension and injustice in 2020, some of the monuments may no longer be at its location. The statues and monuments may be located at the exact address, intersections or in the vicinity.

Note: Interviews with artists were not edited to preserve the artist's voice and authenticity.

Library of Congress Cataloging Number – in- Publication Data has been applied for.

ISBN: 978-1-7354580-1-4

PRINTED IN THE UNITED STATES OF AMERICA.

IN MEMORY OF

Thomas Gibson, father
Jasmyn Lilly Robertson, niece
Ruth Cunningham, grandmother
Eddie Cunningham, grandfather

I love and miss you very much.

CONTENTS

ACKNOWLEDGEMENTS

My mother, Lilly Gibson; sister, Lilly Chapman; son, Receo Thomas Gibson; nephews, Jason and Jayden Robertson; niece, Laila Robertson; daughter-in-law, Alesia Hernandez; grandson, Torah Gibson; great niece, Remi Robertson; great nephew, Avery Robertson; aunts, Katie Luther, Apreal Williamson, Minnie and uncle, Mike Brady. Thank you all for your love, encouragement, and support in my passion to educate African American history. I love you!!!!!!

I would like to thank Charron Monaye, Tammy Denease, Rhonda Thomas, Dr. Kasey Agee and Qiana Earley for your advice, encouragement, and motivating me to write this book.

Special thanks to the following amazing and talented artists: Anthony Peyton Porter, Debra Hand, Frederick Hightower, George Nock, Nijel Binns, Sheleen Jones, Vinnie Bagwell, and Vixon Sullivan. Thank you for taking the time to share your knowledge and experience to aid in my pursuit to educate the importance of public art.

A BIG THANK YOU to the most AWESOME educators I had the honor and pleasure of being their student in the classroom and/or traveling abroad: Chicago State University: Dr. Kim L. Dulaney, Dr. Kelly Ellis, Dr. Kelly Harris, Dr. Wolanyo Kpo, the late Dr. Bart McSwine, the late Prof. Theodore Merriweather and Dr. Saidou Mohamed N'Daou; Howard University: Dr. Mario Beatty and Dr. Greg Carr.

Thank you for the amazing lectures. I have learned and benefited so much from each one of you. You all are the reason I travel to educate and inspire others about the importance of African American history.

Sincere thanks to Ms. Tiffany Hope and Ms. Stephanie Lewis-Ebu for the opportunity of a lifetime to go to Africa. Thank you for making my dream into a reality.

INTRODUCTION

M y travels to locate and document African American statues and monuments started before the 2017 racist incident, where hundreds of tiki torch white supremacist marched at the University of Virginia campus in Charlottesville, VA, fueled with hate chanting "Jews will not replace us" and "Blood and soil" over the removal of the Robert E. Lee statue.

Coincidentally, I attended a conference at UVA-Charlottesville, just weeks after the incident. Early one morning, I went to the Robert E. Lee statue, dedicated in 1924 during the Jim Crow era, at Emancipation Park (formerly Lee Park). The statue was draped over with a shroud for protection and has been vandalized several times over the years. As I stood looking up at the estimated 26 feet tall statue, I felt the racism and intimidating presence that may offend some people. As long as these Confederate statues and flags continue to remain, there will be an increase of rallying points for a white supremacist to ignore the Confederate's soldier's legacy of slavery and racism and glorify their valor. It is a reminder that these monuments are a sign of oppression, fear, and hate when African Americans demanded for equality to be treated with dignity and respect.

The motive of "Continuing the Legacy – African American Monuments and Statues" is to honor prominent African Americans, past and present, who have contributed to civil rights, sports, inventions, politics, and community activism that have statues across the United States. These statues and

3

monuments can be found in colleges, universities, schools, national parks, state capitols, museums, and even cemeteries.

Through my travels, I have located 500+ statues and monuments and only 120 were designed by African American artists. It is imperative to support and learn about these amazing artists' hard work and quality of craftsmanship to preserve and honor African American heritage that will last a lifetime.

Locate statues and monuments in your community. Planning a vacation or family reunion? Plan a day to visit historical sites and locate public art. Look at the structure, detail, quality, appearance, locate the name of the sculptor who designed the statue and research the sculptor's background.

Public art is an important source to immerse yourself and appreciate the stellar beauty of outdoor exhibitions that tell the stories about local culture and history.

MY MONUMENTAL JOURNEY

August 2010–My journey started with a 14-day trip to Egypt in 2010. For several years prior, I kept telling myself, "I'm going to Africa," and finally, it became a reality. The over 15 hours I spent on Flight #986 were filled with excitement, anticipation, and no sleep as I awaited to arrive in Cairo, Egypt.

When I stepped closer to the doors in the line to get off the plane, the brightness of the Africa sun beamed on my face. The heat was brutal but I absorbed the intense warmth because I was finally in Africa!!!!!

I stood on the airplane stairs waiting impatiently to get off and stared at the ground. It felt like a dream because I have always nursed the ambition of being on African soil someday.

While I walked down the stairs, it felt like my body was in slow motion. I walked and stared at the ground. My heart raced and pounded so fast that I thought I was going to pass out. When my feet touched the Africa soil and I heard those beautiful words of our welcome party, "Welcome home, my sister," my mind and body felt like an Energizer bunny with fresh batteries in my back. It took all of my energy to contain myself and managed a simple smile to show my excitement.

That moment started two weeks of travel through Egypt with faculty and students from Chicago State University, Howard University, Miles College, and Northeastern Illinois

University. It was an amazing experience even though my luggage was lost for two days. Though I was disappointed, I wasn't going to let the devil steal my joy because **"I was finally in AFRICA!!!!!!"**

The beauty of Egypt and its amazing scenery, architecture, and people left me speechless. We were able to visit many sites and memorable locations through Egypt. A few notable highlights of the trip were the tours of The Great Sphinx, The Egyptian Museum, The Pyramid of Kufu, The Valley of the Kings, Queens and Nobles, Hathsepsut's Temple, The Colossi of Memnon, and The Temple of Ramses II.

For me, the greatest experiences I had was jumping into the Nile River, climbing The Pyramids of Giza, and the camel ride. This trip changed my life and inspired me so much to explore other African countries. Since then, I have traveled to Ghana, Senegal, Gambia, South Africa, Tanzania, Rwanda, Zimbabwe, and Zanzibar.

When someone asks me what my favorite country in Africa is, I usually tell them that it has to be my first trip in 2010 to Egypt.

Being exposed to African and African American culture, I realized that I view the world as a classroom. I wanted to travel the world. My passion for traveling means that I get to educate myself globally and try as much as I can to meet amazing people during my journey. I get so much excitement when I plan my next adventure and I also look forward to passing on the information I have learned to the next generation.

For the past 10 years, I have traveled throughout the United States and internationally, locating and documenting African American historical sites that have been forgotten. These travels have highlighted America's refusal to reckon with slavery and economic injustices and trauma against African Americans.

I have traveled to the historical homes of Frederick Douglass, W.E.B. Dubois, Mary McCleod Bethune, Marian Anderson, Paul Laurence Dunbar, Muhammad Ali, and

Aurelia S. Browder. I have located historical markers, monuments, slave cemeteries, and met civil rights activists along the way.

To date, I have visited over 50 slave plantations and slept in slave cabins to honor the ancestors whose shoulders I stand on. I have used my experiences as active learning engagements to educate myself, others and to stress the fact that these sacred places matter as an important part of not just my history but American history.

There have been times when I have visited plantations and heard tour guides say that "slaves were treated well." In anger and disbelief, I asked in response, "What do you mean by treated well?"

Their responses usually were, "They weren't punished and lashed... or, they kept the families together...or, they were able to go to neighboring plantations to visit family members..." and other things like that. When I challenge the guides' absurd answers, I am met with intimidation, nervousness, hesitation, and/or deflection.

I believe this is a serious and detrimental problem we face when visiting slave plantations in search of history. The narrative the tour guides give sugarcoats the reality of the torments and agony our ancestors went through. While visiting plantations, I have encountered tour guides call the enslaved that toiled in the cotton (King Cotton), sugar (White Gold), rice and/or tobacco fields workers and the slave cabins/quarters are called duplexes. On my visit to Andrew Jackson's Hermitage, before entering the grounds, there are banners with words that describe Jackson as a Hero, President, Statesman, and Legend. The historical site fails to add another adjective: Slave Owner.

These distinctions serve as forms of historical amnesia, cultural genocide and sugarcoat versions of slavery to make some people feel comfortable while attempting to cover up hundreds of years of traumatic abuse of an entire race.

When I visit plantations, I see two worlds; the world of the enslaved and the world of the slave owner. Plantation tour guides give detailed and thorough historical information about the "Big House" and most of the time only provide self-guided tours of the enslaved cabins.

When I stand in front of a "Big House," I usually see a huge mansion with large white columns, bright green lush manicured lawns, oak trees, that are hundreds of years old cascading over one another with beautiful flowers such as geraniums, magnolias, azaleas, and lilies. If the "Big House" was made out of brick, I always look to see if I could find any enslaved fingerprints.

Inside the "Big House," the tour guide talks about the beauty of the house, and the oohs and aahs are always heard from the visitors. You would see portraits of the slave owner and his family displayed throughout the house with high ceilings, chandeliers, spiral stairs, and several rooms that you would see in magazines such as Better Homes and Gardens.

While walking on the grounds, I think of the enslaved women and men that were forced to work for free and expected to meet every demand of the "Massa" and "Mistress" of the "Big House." The enslaved had to endure mental, physical, and sexual abuse regularly.

The main reason I visit slave plantations is not just to admire the beauty of the grounds or the "Big House," but to see the ugliness behind the "Big House" where enslaved men, women, and children were kept in bondage.

The slave quarters that I've visited were, at times, several feet away from the "Big House." When I saw an original slave cabin, the first thing that came to mind was a question: How did they endure a lifetime in bondage under those conditions? When I stepped inside an original cabin, I looked up at the ceiling, touched the deteriorated walls, and looked at the floors that my ancestors walked, cried, and slept on.

I've had the opportunity to experience what it's like to sleep in slave quarters with The Slave Dwelling Project. I have spent the night on a wooden or dirt floor in a sleeping bag in complete darkness. Right in there, I couldn't see my hand in front of my face. I heard the wind through the cracks in the walls and the sounds of wild animals throughout the night. Every night, there I was either sweating profusely from the nighttime heat, bitten by hungry mosquitos, freezing, tossing and turning, not getting a wink of sleep.

One experience that brought me to tears was an overnight stay at a particular plantation. I was around the campfire with historians, preservationists, and descendants of slaves. It was around midnight, and while we were in deep conversation, in the distance, I heard music coming from the Big House. I believe it was a wedding reception. My mind went to that of an enslaved and immediately, a question popped in my head, "what would I be doing if I were my ancestors?" I would either be thinking of a strategy to escape to freedom or try to sleep before getting up early the next morning to toil in the field. The reality is that there is loud music and a party going on at the Big House and here they were enslaved.

It's imperative that these sacred grounds are preserved and the history of the enslaved ancestor's story be told because they did not only provide economic wealth for the slave owner and his family but the economic fabric of the United States. My ancestors provided me the freedom and opportunity to travel and retrace a part of this painful chapter in history. We absolutely can't forget about slavery. We can't afford to do that. Slavery is a permanent and embedded stain in American history. There are 400+ years of tragedies and achievements that have contributed to the foundation of this country.

I found throughout my travels, the deliberate intent to overlook the history of slavery to make it more palatable for the masses. Black history has been disrespected, withheld, whitewashed, used and abused to preserve the fallacies and deception of the bondage of our ancestors. The Titanic, Holocaust, and 9/11 will never be forgotten. Neither should the cruelty and the lasting effects of slavery.

I had the opportunity to volunteer in an archaeology program at James Madison's Montpelier in Virginia, where

I learned excavation from Matthew Reeves, Director of Archaeology & Landscape Restoration.

It was an amazing experience sifting through the dirt and recovering artifacts around the South Yard kitchen, where the enslaved community lived and toiled at Montpelier. I found animal teeth, bones, buttons, needles, a toothbrush, and pieces of broken plates that have been buried for centuries. It was very emotional knowing that the last person that touched these items was more than likely an enslaved individual.

For the past couple of years, I have been involved in "Behind The Big House" Tour in Holly Springs, MS, the birthplace of journalist and anti-lynching activist, my shero, Ida B. Wells.

Behind the Big House was developed to interpreting slavery by private homeowners, who open slave houses on their property to the public for interpreters, such as myself, to educate tourists and students the story of the enslaved men, women, and children who were kept and toiled in Holly Springs. The program was formed in 2012 by Chelius Carter and Jenifer Eggleston, who bought the Hugh Craft House. Built in 1851, Hugh Craft House is locally recognized as the first of the "big houses" during the town's initially affluence preceding the King Cotton era of the late 1850s.

Hugh Craft House had slave quarters with a detached kitchen. The 1860 Marshall County Slave Census shows nine enslaved people at the house.

The program is run through Preserve Marshall County and Holly Springs Inc., which gets its funding from the Mississippi Humanities Council, the Mississippi Development Authority, the Mississippi Hills National Heritage Area, and the Holly Springs Tourism and Recreation Bureau.

I had the honor of working with Culinary Historian Michael W. Twitty, author of "The Cooking Gene," earning him the 2018 James Beard Award's Book of the Year.

He's made some fantastic dishes such as okra stew, fried chicken, homemade biscuits, red field pies, rabbit, dumplings, country captain, sweet potato cornbread, etc.

I always look forward to not only eating Twitty's mouthwatering dishes, but he would put me to work in the kitchen. It was intimidating when he gave me instructions on how to prep a dish and look at him like he was speaking a foreign language lol. He was very patient with me, and he showed me how to make homemade biscuits and pie crust.

Joseph McGill, founder of The Slave Dwelling Project, Inc., for ten years, has been providing insight into the lives of enslaved men, women and children who lived and toiled on the site for ten years. McGill has slept in 100+ slave dwellings to raise awareness of the importance of preserving these structures and the history of slavery. Artisan Wayne Jones, and Dale DeBerry, provided 19th-century brick making demonstrations. A plantation I visited in South Carolina told me that enslaved brickmakers had to make 3,000 bricks per day.

I had the amazing opportunity to interpret the role of an enslaved laundress and demonstrate the daunting and grueling task of doing laundry that took several days to complete with Behind the Big House Tour and in the classroom.

The enslaved laundress did all the laundry for the slaveowner's family. She did the bedding, clothes, curtains, table linen, drapes, etc. Monday was "Wash Day." She had to sort, bat, boil, wash, rinse, air dry, iron, mend and fold. There was no way that one laundress can do all the laundry. She would have other women and children to help her with this challenging task. It would take several days to do the laundry.

I showed the students how lye soap and indigo were made by hand. The laundress would get chemical burns making the lye soap.

Children also helped the laundress. They had to get buckets of clean water using a shoulder yoke. There may be a well close around, or they would have to walk several miles to a river to get water.

The students had never seen a washboard before. I showed them how to wash with a washboard and iron using a sad iron. The iron would weigh between five to nine pounds or more, and the laundress arms would get sore and tired. The iron would be heated on a plate or close to a fire. When the iron gets hot, the handle gets heated as well. The laundress would have to use a thick cloth or rag to pick up the iron. Sometimes, the laundress would get burns and blisters on their hands.

I love telling the students about the life and legacy of Oseola McCarty. She was a washerwoman. Raised by her grandmother and aunt, they taught her how to wash clothes and iron.

As a child, when she finished school, she would go home and wash and iron. The money she got paid for washing and ironing, she would stash her money in her doll buggy.

In the 1960s, she purchased a washer and dryer, thinking it would be easier for her to do her job. The clothes were not cleaned as she liked, and the whites turned a yellowish color. She got rid of her washer and dryer and went back to the Maid-Rite washboard.

In 1995, she retired due to decades of washing and ironing; she developed arthritis. When she retired, she saved $280,000. She donated 10% to her church, 30% to family, and 60% to the University of Southern Mississippi. When Ms. McCarty was a child, the university was segregated. She remembered walking pass the university and was not allowed to attend. She wanted her money to be a scholarship and be given to African American students who needed financial help. Ms. McCarty donated $150,000 to the University of Southern Mississippi.

The first Oseola McCarty Scholarship went to Stephanie Bullock. She received $1,000.00. Ms. McCarty and Ms. Bullock became real close. Ms. Bullock invited Ms. McCarty to her college graduation.

Ms. McCarty became an instant celebrity. She received an honorary degree from the University of Southern Mississippi, an honorary doctorate degree from Harvard University, and President Bill Clinton awarded Ms. McCarty the Presidential Citizen Award. She was asked whether she has any regrets, and her response was, "I wish I could have gave more."

Ms. McCarty died September 26, 1999, and buried at Highland Cemetery in Hattiesburg, MS. There is a park in her name, and her home will be a future museum.

The students enjoyed the presentation. I passionately told the students the importance of getting an education and the generosity of Ms. McCarty. She had a 6th-grade education, but she unselfishly gave the majority of her savings to students that needed financial assistance to get the education to be successful in their future career endeavors.

Another adventurous part of my journey was going to cemeteries to pay respect to ancestors that are gone but not forgotten. I view it as an outdoor museum full of history. Some people think it's scary, but you can learn so much from a gravesite. Cemetery tours have become popular for tourists. I have seen gravesites at some unique locations like behind a hotel, an apartment complex, on the median, an expressway, and in the middle of a road. I have seen some of the most unique headstones and items left by visitors such as coins, hats, weed, beer bottles, sporting goods, candles, cigars, photos, underwear, and a rake, just to name a few.

I have located some well-maintained African American cemeteries, but some of the cemeteries have overgrown grass, trees, trash, used tires, old mattresses, and furniture. Some of the toppled headstones, neglected, abandoned, and depressing graves were of prominent African American politicians, veterans, activists, celebrities, and loved ones with unmarked graves or marked by a simple stone.

Majority of these old historical cemeteries do not have the funding to clean and restore them, so family members have to care for their loved ones grave and at times with the assistance of a volunteer worker. I had the opportunity to volunteer for a couple of hours at a historical African American cemetery incorporated in 1875 in Houston, Texas. There was a descendent that had a loved one buried at the cemetery and was mowing the grounds when he welcomed me and provided me with information on the history of the first incorporated African American cemetery in Houston. The hurricane damage resulted in fallen trees and lots of debris that needed to be removed.

I have seen the vandalism on headstones. Fred Hampton, Chairman of the Illinois Black Panther Party was assassinated along with Mark Clark by the Chicago police on December 4, 1969. Hampton is buried in Louisiana and his headstone is peppered with bullets. Even in death, Hampton is still a threat.

Jimmie Lee Jackson was shot in the stomach by a police officer during a peaceful voting rights march in Selma, AL, February 18, 1965. Jackson died on February 26, 1965. His death sparked the Selma to Montgomery march. Jackson is buried at Heard Cemetery near Marion, AL. His headstone is riddled with bullets.

It's important to preserve, appreciate, and understand the rich history of these sacred cemeteries and to protect it from vandalism, commercial development and gentrification. Black graves are historical markers for black lives. Black Graves Matter!

Going to several cemeteries and going through my mother's photo album of obituaries, Bibles and locating the resting place of my ancestors directed my travels to Vaiden, MS. It was truly an amazing experience. It was great looking at the symbols and the meanings on the headstones, pouring libation in memory and honoring my ancestors who have paved the path that I walk to continue their legacy.

One of my difficult journeys was locating where African American men, women, and children were lynched. It started when I went to Jasper, TX, where James Byrd was dragged for 2-3 miles by three white supremacists. Byrd's body parts and personal belongings were stretched for about 2-3 miles. His head was found in a ditch, torso, arm, pieces of his flesh, dentures, keys, hat, and wallet were also found. The rest of his remains were left at an African American church and cemetery. His grave is surrounded by a fence due to vandalism.

Driving down Huff Creek Road & Co Rd 278, where Byrd was dragged, I thought to myself that this could have been my father, uncle, brother, husband, son, or friend. This prompted me to locate historical markers and gravesites of African American victims who were lynched. The fact that some people commemorated this horrific act as a major event dressed in their finest clothing having barbeques, sending postcards of pictures of African American men, women, and children hanging from a telephone pole, lamppost or tree and saving their charred body parts as souvenirs was very disturbing and prompt me to find out the stories of these human beings who were victimized.

EJI researchers documented 4,075 racial terror lynchings of African Americans in Alabama, Arkansas, Florida, Georgia, Kentucky, Louisiana, Mississippi, North Carolina, South Carolina, Tennessee, Texas, and Virginia between 1877 and 1950—at least 800 more lynchings of Black people in these states than previously reported in the most comprehensive work done on lynching to date.

I attended the grand opening of The National Memorial for Peace and Justice in Montgomery, AL, on April 26, 2019. Seeing the 800 six-foot steel monuments of the names of 4,400 African American men, women, and children that were lynched, I kept hearing the haunting song in my mind "Strange Fruit" by Billie Holiday.

Southern trees bear a strange fruit,
Blood on the leaves and blood at the root,
Black body swinging in the Southern breeze,
Strange fruit hanging from the poplar trees.
Pastoral scene of the gallant South,
The bulging eyes and the twisted mouth,

Scent of magnolia sweet and fresh,
And the sudden smell of burning flesh!
Here is a fruit for the crows to pluck,
For the rain to gather, for the wind to suck,
For the sun to rot, for a tree to drop,
Here is a strange and bitter crop.

At the memorial, I met two sisters. Their great grandfather, Rev. Arthur St. Clair was shot and killed by a group of men for officiating the marriage of an interracial couple (David James, who was black and Lizzy Day, who was white) on June 1877 in Hernando County, FL, while he was returning from a meeting for his fourth run for the State House at Dade City.

St. Clair was a major figure in reconstruction politics. He held several offices including "voter registrar, deputy sheriff, county commissioner, captain in the state militia, delegate to the 1876 Republican state convention and three-time Republican nominee for the State House."

My experience attending the memorial was very emotional. Seeing the names of innocent black lives that were tortured and lynched provided a direct connection to the injustices that are still prevalent today. There were tears, hugging, holding hands amongst the visitors. When it started to rain heavily, it heightened the gravity of the emotions I was feeling because I truly believe it was the tears of joy from the ancestors to finally reclaim and honor their memory.

The following are just a few sites I have visited to trace the individuals who lost their lives to lynching:

1892–Ida B. Wells' friends, Thomas Moss, Calvin McDowell, and Will Stewart owners of People's Grocery, were lynched by a white mob because a white grocer named William Barrett found his business was declining due to the success of the black men's grocery store. **Marker – Memphis, TN; Grave and Marker – Zion Christian Cemetery, Memphis, TN**

1906–Ed Johnson was accused of raping a white woman, Nevada Taylor, in Chattanooga, TN. A mob broke into the jail and hung Johnson. His last words were, "God Bless You All. I Am A Innocent Man." His conviction was posthumously vacated in 2000. **Grave – Pleasant Gardens Cemetery, Ridgeside, TN**

1906–Henry Davis is documented as the last man lynched in Annapolis, MD. He was shot over 100 times for allegedly assaulting a white woman. **Marker–Brewer Hill Cemetery, Annapolis, MD**

1908–William Miller, a coal miner, was lynched by a white mob in Brighton, AL, for advocating for better wages for black coal miners and accused of bombing a home. **Marker – Brighton, AL**

1908 – Mabel Hallam, a white woman, lied that she was raped by a black man, George Richardson, a black man. That sparked the Springfield, IL Race Riot. Business owners, Scott Burton (59-year old barbershop owner) and William Donnegan (84-year old shoemaker) were lynched as a result. Burton was shot four times, hanged and mutilated. Donnegan was taken from his home, hanged from a tree, stabbed and throat slashed. Hallam admitted she fabricated the accusation. **Graves – Oak Ridge Cemetery, Springfield, IL**

1917–Ell Persons was lynched in his 50s. He was accused of raping a white girl, Antoinette Rappel. He was beaten into a confession, burned alive, and dismembered in front of thousands of spectators. Food was sold at the lynching. **Marker – Memphis, TN**

1918–Mary Turner was eight months pregnant when she was lynched for speaking out about the lynching of her husband. An angry white mob lynched, shot, burn and cut her fetus out of her stomach. Mary Turner Memorial Marker, where she was lynched, has been riddled with bullets several times. I see this too many times during my travels where African American historical markers, gravesites, and landmarks are vandalized. **Marker–Lowndes County, Georgia**

1919 – Eugene Williams accidentally crossed over an invisible line at a segregated beach in Chicago. White beachgoers threw rocks at Williams, causing him to drown. That incident sparked the 1919 Chicago Race Riot. **Marker – Chicago, IL; Grave – Lincoln Cemetery, Chicago, IL**

1920–Julius "July" Perry, businessman and landowner, was beaten, shot and lynched by a white mob for getting African Americans to vote on Election Day in Ocoee, FL. **Marker Orlando, FL; Grave – Greenwood Cemetery, Orlando, FL**

1920–Elias Clayton, Elmer Jackson, and Isaac McGhie, who was employed by the John Robinson Circus, were lynched for being accused of raping a white woman, Irene Tuskan. **Monument – Duluth, MN; Graves – Park Hill Cemetery, Duluth, MN**

1923–James T. Scott was lynched. He was wrongfully accused of raping a 14-year-old girl, Regina Almstedt. His case never went to trial. A white mob dragged him out of jail and hung him from the Stewart Road bridge in Missouri. No one was convicted of the crime. **Monument – Columbia, MO; Grave – Columbia Cemetery, Columbia, MO**

1944–George Stinney was accused of killing two white sisters, Amie Betty June and Mary Emma, in Pinewood, SC. He was the youngest person, age 14, to be executed by the electric chair. In 2014, his conviction was vacated. **Marker–Alcolu, SC**

1947–Willie Earle was the last man lynched recorded in South Carolina. He was accused of killing a white cab driver he vehemently stated he did not commit. Earle was beaten, mutilated, and shot to death by an angry mob. **Marker – Stolen in Greenville, SC; Grave – Abel Baptist Church Cemetery, Clemson, SC**

1947–Elmore Bolling was shot to death by jealous whites because he was a successful entrepreneur. He owned a trucking business, managed a farm, and ran a general store. He gave back to the community and hired African Americans. The murderers were never indicted. **Marker–Lowndesboro, AL**

1954–Isadore Banks, a landowner of over 1,000 acres of land, who helped to bring the first black operated cotton gin to Memphis was lynched, mutilated, and set on fire because of his success. **Billboard – Near Marion, AR on Interstate 55; Grave – Marion Memorial Cemetery, Marion, AR**

1955–Carolyn Bryant accused Emmett Till of some type of sexual-oriented violation at her husband's store in Money, MS. Decades later, she recanted her story. **Markers – Money, Sumner, Glendora and Greenwood, MS; Grave – Burr Oak Cemetery, Alsip, IL**

1959–Mack Charles Parker, a veteran, was lynched. He was accused of raping a white woman. He pleaded not guilty. A white mob, dragged Parker from his jail cell shot him, weighted his body with chains, and threw it into the river. His body was found after 10 days. **Grave – Big Quarters Cemetery, Lumberton, MS**

1985–Timothy Brian Cole, veteran and a law student at Texas Tech University was wrongfully accused and convicted of raping a white woman, Michele Milan, in Lubbock, TX. He died in prison in 1999 and was posthumously vacated in

2009. In 2015, Texas Tech University awarded a posthumous honorary law and social justice degree to Cole. **Marker and Grave – Mount Olive Cemetery, Fort Worth, TX**

As a travel historian, it's important to me to educate and share valuable historical facts about African Americans who have contributed to the foundation of the United States. Slavery, lynchings, segregation are a constant reminder of a period that is painful in American history. It is important to highlight black history not just in February, but every month of the year.

MONUMENTAL CONTROVERSY

Black history is multifaceted with a multitude of layers. Discussions can span from the inception of slavery and the lynching of Black bodies to the assassination of great Black leaders and the proper place of African American history in school books. One of the noted dialogues knitted throughout history is the symbolism of Confederate monuments in cities across the nation. According to the Southern Poverty Law Center (SPLC), there are presently 1,747 Confederate monuments in public places that honor Confederate leaders, soldiers or the Confederate States of America. These works include flags, parks, schools, military bases and other public spaces, with 780 of them being statues located in 23 states.

Of course, there are two sides to the argument regarding the display of confederate works. On one end, those for the towering bronze statues dispute that tearing them down will result in the erasure of the southern history, pride and heritage of the country. However, those on the opposing side believe that all of these monuments are a symbol of hatred and overlooks the long-standing history of racism in the U.S.—past and present.

To see the bigger picture, the textbook history and heritage of the country must come under question and scrutiny. The spirit of deep-rooted white supremacy is entrenched in each statue that stands tall over African American neighborhoods, on the lawn of educational institutions, and at the center of community parks. It is clear that without the understanding of why these monuments were erected in the first place and what they represent to African Americans, the ongoing battle to remove these symbols of racism, bigotry, and hatred will continue to fall on deaf ears.

THE ROAD TO REMOVAL

Over the years, there have been cries to have Confederate monuments removed and either put into storage or exhibited in museums. But one particular tragedy ultimately became the start of a movement. On June 17th, 2015, Dylann Roof attended Bible study at the historic A.M.E. Church in Charleston, North Carolina—a place of worship known for its iconic presence during the civil rights movement. That evening, he murdered nine African Americans in the name of causing a "race war." Prior to his actions, he was indoctrinated into a white supremacy group online and pictures of Roof surfaced toting the Confederate battle flag. Contrary to what he set out to do, his actions incited a movement to remove the flag from public places. Simultaneously, the movement evolved into taking a deeper look into the many other symbols nationally that remain front and center.

As the talks started to die down, the controversy started to simmer once again in 2017 after the Unite The Right rally, where white nationalists marched against the removal of a General Robert E. Lee statue in Charlottesville, Virginia. The clash between nationalists and protesters resulted in the death of a protester, several others injured, and violent confrontations with demonstrators.

The murder of George Floyd on May 25th, 2020 was the beginning of an uprising that has revived the discussion behind confederate monuments and pushed it along even further. The nation and the world watched in horror as a video captured Floyd's murder at the knee of a police officer in Minneapolis, Minnesota. As a result, the protests across the world for inequity and police brutality reactivated the same conversation detested by nationalists.

These monumental events are embedded in history and add to the important discussion at hand. In some cities, actions speak for themselves as necessary steps have been taken to remove monuments, while others protected by civic leaders have made the swift decision to pass laws to protect them. Either way, the heated conversation continues.

TRUTHS BEHIND THE LOST CAUSE MYTH VS THE CIVIL WAR

The ongoing debate is about how Confederate statues came to stem from two totally different perspectives. Nationalists and white southerners tend to lean towards the Lost Cause myth; a storied glorification of the Old South. They see the Civil War as a heroic fight that took place to preserve sovereignty, division of the states and their rights. However, the stance historians take derives from facts which demonstrate that the Civil War was a battle clearly fought to reign supreme over African Americans and keep slavery intact. The white-washed version of what transpired depicts a time when southerners were in power and had control and domination over the black populace while they were happy—as slaves.

By 1910, the south had embraced their simplified version of the Civil War and Confederate statues were erected en masse throughout the states. Still, the predominant era in the serge of statues occurred between 1890 and 1920, a mere 30 years after the end of the Civil War. These cast interpretations were all depictions of generals and soldiers of the Confederacy. During this time, Jim Crow laws were in effect. We must keep in mind that the laws and state constitutional provisions were set to segregate Blacks and Whites in public spaces, public transportation, schools, restaurants, restrooms, and drinking fountains, essentially keeping first-generation African Americans who were born outside of slavery "in their place." To date, there are still many monuments standing tall over neighborhoods and plaques that are prominently seen around cities.

THE VANDALIZING AND DISRESPECT OF AFRICAN AMERICAN STATUES

African American monuments have also been caught in the crossfire during times of civil unrest and turbulence. Throughout the years, many African American monuments have been victim to vandalization and defacing. While very few have been listed as pranks, the majority of cases have been racially-motivated or race-related. Here is a shortlist of some of the monuments that have been vandalized in some way over the years.

Year: 2020
Where: Richmond, VA
Artist: Paul DiPasquale

Who: Arthur Ashe–an African American professional tennis player, writer, commentator, civil rights supporter and philanthropist. He is the first black man to win the Australian Open, U.S. Open and Wimbledon. Ashe was inducted into the International Tennis Hall of Fame in 1985.

Why: This monument was created to celebrate the achievements and legacy of Arthur Ashe and was meticulously placed along Monument Avenue to counterbalance the number of Confederate statues already standing.

Occurrence: Arthur Ashe statue was vandalized with WLM (White Live Matter) spray painted across the pedestal in bright blue letters.

Year: 2020
Where: Boston, MA
Artist: Augustus Saint-Gaudens

Who: Robert Gould Shaw and the 54th Regiment Memorial–a memorial dedicated to the African Americans who served in the Civil War. The 54th Regiment was the first African American volunteer infantry unit that fought after Abraham Lincoln signed the Emancipation Proclamation. Colonel Robert Gould Shaw inspired the men to join the war to fight for freedom. The unit fought a major battle at Fort Wagner, where Colonel Robert Gould and many of his men were killed. Others who were captured in combat were either killed or enslaved. The story of the unit and colonel are portrayed in the 1989 movie, Glory. This is noted as the first civic monument to mark the gallantry of the African American soldiers.

Why: The memorial is a tribute to Colonel Robert Gould Shaw and members of the 54th Regiment. It depicts their march down Beacon Street to fight in the South on May 28th, 1963.

Occurrence: The memorial, in the middle of a $3 million restoration, was spray painted with profanity on the back of the monument.

Year: 2019
Where: Chapel Hill, NC
Artist: Do-Ho Suh

Who: Unsung Founders' Memorial at the University of North Carolina–erected in 2005, the memorial was a gift from the graduating class of 2002 to honor the unsung founders of the university. The senior class raised $54,000, exceeding their initial goal of $40,000. The remaining balance was contributed by students, friends of the university and parents. The full inscription reads: "The Class of 2002 honors the University's unsung founders – the people of color bond and free – who helped build the Carolina that we cherish today."

Why: Though the inscription omits the words "Black" or "slaves", it is clear via the artist's interpretation and design that the memorial is a tribute to the enslaved Black people who helped to build the UNC campus.

Occurrence: Racist language was found on Unsung Founders' Memorial at the University of North Carolina at Chapel Hill.

Year: 2019
Where: Winter Park, FL
Artist: Rigoberto Torres

Who: Tuskegee Airman, Richard Hall, Jr.–Richard Hall, Jr. served in World War II as part of the Tuskegee Airmen "Red Tails." He was one of 996 African American pilots and 15,000 ground personnel who served in the U.S. Air Force's all Black units during World War II; the first in the history of the U.S. Hall reported to Tuskegee, Alabama, for training. He then joined the 332nd Fighter Group and 477th Composite Group. The latter included the 99th Fighter Squadron and the 617th Bomber Squadron.

Occurrence: The statue was struck, creating a large hole in the abdominal area of the statue. It has since been repaired and restored as of May 2019.

Year: 2018
Where: Rochester, NY
Artist: Olivia Kim

Who: Frederick Douglass – a writer, abolitionist and orator. He became a national leader after escaping slavery. Douglass was the first Black man to be nominated for Vice President of the United States. He wrote several books and was an active supporter of civil rights for all and the abolition of slavery.

Why: The statue was one of a series to commemorate the 200th birthday of Frederick Douglass. This endeavor was organized by the Re-energizing the Legacy of Frederick Douglass Committee.

Occurrence: The two vandalists, John R. Boedicker and Charles J. Milks, who were out in a drunken stupor, broke the statue at the foundation and were attempting to carry it offsite as a prank.

Year: 2018
Where: New York City, NY
Artist: Rodney Leon & AARIS Architects

Who: African Burial Ground Monument

Why: Established in 2009, the monument sits on a burial ground, containing over 15,000 skeletal remains of free and enslaved African Americans from the 17th and 18th centuries from New York. The site also integrates 7 different elements to mark and celebrate the ancestors buried there. It is considered a sacred site.

Occurrence: It was defaced with the word "kill" and a racial slur, suggesting Black people should be killed.

Year: 2016
Where: Tampa, FL
Artist: Linda Ackley

Who: Martin Luther King, Jr. – a minister and prominent leader of the civil rights movement. He won the Nobel Peace Prize for battling injustice in racial inequality via a non-violent movement and helped to organize the Selma to Montgomery marches. His iconic "I Have A Dream" speech is a notable moment in history, which took place on the Lincoln Memorial steps. Dr. King was assassinated on April 4th, 1968 in Memphis, Tennessee.

Why: The bust is located in a plaza which was dedicated to Martin Luther King Jr. with a push by the Black Student Union in 1982. It resided in the middle of the university campus since 1996.

Occurrence: MAGA hat was placed on the Martin Luther King, Jr. bust at the University of South Florida.

Year: 2016
Where: Wichita, KS
Artist: Georgia Gerber

Who: Dockum Sit-in Sculpture

Why: The monument commemorates the historic Dockum Sit-in in 1958. It was considered the first successful lunch counter sit-in in the U.S as an effort to end segregation. Started by Carol Parks-Hahn and her cousin Ron Walters, the sit-in took place over a 3-week span with their friends. Peacefully, they attended lunch at the counter every day while they were continuously refused service. On August 11th, 1958, they were finally served once the owner conceded he was losing too much money.

Occurrence: Orange graffiti on the Wichita Kansas Dockum Drug Store statue.

Year: 2015
Where: Oxford, MS
Artist: Rod Moorhead

Who: James Meredith–inspired by the inaugural speech by JFK, Meredith applied to the university to put pressure on the Kennedy's administration to implement a plan of action for African American civil rights. He also organized the March Against Fear, known as the largest civil rights marches in Mississippi.

Why: Meredith became the first African American to integrate the University of Mississippi campus in 1962.

Occurrence: Noose and old Georgia State flag with the Confederate battle emblem draped around the neck of the James Meredith statue at the University of Mississippi.

CONFEDERATE MONUMENTS BEING TORN DOWN

The ongoing battle and discussion to remove Confederate statues continue to take place, but the outrage outweighs patience from those continuously vying for change. In the midst of protests for social injustice and police brutality, there have been many monuments depicting Confederate leaders that have been vandalized, toppled or slated for removal.

Here is an in-depth list of monuments that have been affected.

Who: Philip Schuyler

Where: Albany, N.Y.

History: Schuyler served in the army as a Major and General. It is argued that without him, the Revolutionary War wouldn't have been won. He was said to be the largest slave owner in Albany. He owned 17 slaves; 13 of whom worked at his mansion and 4 worked on his farm in Saratoga County. The monument is displayed in front of Albany City Hall.

Slated for Removal: On June 11th, 2020, Mayor Kathy Sheehan signed an executive order to have the monument removed. It will then be stored in a museum or given to an institution.[17]

Who: Appomattox

Where: Alexandria, VA

History: The monument has been in place for 131 years at the intersection of South Washington Street and Prince Street in the Old Town of Alexandria. A sculpted Confederate soldier stands facing south viewing the outcome of the battle Appomattox Court House; the surrender of General Robert E. Lee to Union General Ulysses S. Grant.

Dismantled: The monument was set for removal in July 2020, but the city decided to remove it in June 2020 due to many statues being vandalized.[18]

Who: Charles Linn

Where: Birmingham, AL

History: Known as a Confederate officer in the Confederate States Navy; the statue was erected in 2013 and placed in Linn Park. He was one of the founders of Birmingham, Alabama, and held particular investments in banking and a wholesale grocery warehouse.

Vandalized: The monument was toppled over on June 2nd, 2020.[19]

Who: Confederate Sailors and Soldiers Monument

Where: Birmingham, AL

History: What originally lay as a concrete plinth in 1864 was later transformed in 1905 to a five-story tall monument to Confederate troops.

Vandalized and Dismantled: Mayor Randall Woodfin and the City Council had the remaining pieces of the obelisk removed in June 2020 with the plinth remaining. The Alabama Attorney General later filed a lawsuit against the city of Alabama, citing the violation of the Alabama Memorial Preservation Act of 2017 which protects this monument. Mayor Woodfin resolved to pay the $25,000 fine to keep civil unrest at bay.[20]

Who: Christopher Columbus

Where: Boston, MA

History: The marble statue was added in 1979. The monument was placed in the Christopher Columbus Waterfront Park, created to honor The Massachusetts State Council's patron, Christopher Columbus. Known to many as the explorer who discovered America, Columbus is also known for his violent treatment and killing of Native Americans. He was a tyrant who paved the way for the trans-Atlantic slave trade. Over the course of years, the statue has a history of being frequently vandalized. Notably, in 2004, when it was inscribed with red paint with the word "murderer," in 2006, when it was beheaded for the first time, and in 2015, when it was spray painted with the words "Black Lives Matter."

Vandalized and Dismantled: The statue in the North End was beheaded by protestors in June 2020. A few days later,

Mayor Marty Wash had it removed from its base and put into storage.[21]

Who: George Washington

Where: Chicago, IL

History: Located on the South Side of Chicago, the monument has been in place since 1904. The statue depicts Washington during the Revolutionary War. A slave owner himself, Washington supported measures put in place to protect slavery.

Vandalized: The statue located in Chicago Washington Park was fitted with a white hood and gown to represent the Klu Klux Klan and spray painted with messages "slave owner" and "God Bless Amerikkka" on the base in June 2020.[22]

Who: Lawrence Sullivan Ross

Where: College Station, TX

History: Ross was a Confederate soldier who served as the governor of Texas. He later became the president of Texas A&M from 1891 until his death in 1898. The monument was dedicated in 1918 on the Texas A&M University campus.

Vandalized: The monument was vandalized with the words "BLM", "racist" and "ACAB" in red graffiti along the base, fitted with a rainbow-colored wig, and red paint was thrown across the face and body of the statue.[23]

Who: Texas Ranger One Riot, One Ranger (Captain Jay Banks)

Where: Dallas, TX

History: Donated to the city in 1963, the monument depicts Captain Jay Banks–who was in charge of a Ranger contingent in 1957, which blocked Black children from enrolling in Mansfield's High School, despite court rulings preventing such actions. He also sided with mobs that were on school premises to keep Black children out.

Dismantled: A decision was made by the Office of Arts and Culture and the airport in June 2020 to remove the statue from Dallas Love Field airport and will be left in storage until a discussion is had over where it can be displayed in a prominent location.[24]

Who: Orville Hubbard

Where: Dearborn, MI

History: Hubbard's monument originally stood outside the city's Old City Hall and was moved in 2015 outside the Dearborn Historical Museum. Known as the longest mayor to serve Dearborn from 1942 to 1978, he liberally used racial slurs and exclusively excluded minorities, especially African Americans.

Dismantled: Dearborn City Council President, Susan Dabaja, announced in June 2020 via Facebook that The Hubbard Family will relocate the monument to Hubbards's gravesite.[25]

Who: Confederate Memorial

Where: Huntsville, TX

History: Erected in 1956 in the midst of racial segregation under Jim Crow laws by the United Daughters of the Confederacy, the monument honored Confederate soldiers on the Walker County Courthouse grounds.

Vandalized: The monument was spray painted in black to cover the Confederate flag and inscription which read, "In memory of our Confederate patriots 1861-1865."[26]

Who: Confederate Monument memorializing Confederate prisoners of war

Where: Indianapolis, IN

History: The monument was originally placed in Greenlawn Cemetery and was moved to Garfield Park in 1928. Public figures connected with the Klu Klux Klan voted to have it moved for more prominent visibility. In 2017, the Indianapolis Parks Board passed a resolution to have the statue removed as soon as funding was secured.

Dismantled: In June 2020, Mayor Joe Hogsett called for its removal and the monument was dismantled. [27]

Who: Confederate monument in Hemming Park

Where: Jacksonville, FL

History: Since 1898, the statue and plaque honored fallen Confederate soldiers. Donated to the state of Florida by Charles C. and Lucy Key Hemming, it was one of the few Jacksonville monuments that survived The Great Fire of 1901—the third-largest fire in the U.S.

Dismantled: In June 2020, Mayor Lenny Curry had the monument removed from the park.[28] Standing at City Hall, Mayor Curry also announced the removal of all Confederate monuments citywide.[29] There is presently no word as to when the transition will start.

CONCLUSION

There are many more Confederate statues on display throughout the states that remain a stark reminder of the racist, bigoted and disparaging past locked into American history. While monuments will continue to chronicle events for a time to come, a shift in the encompassing focus would redirect everyone's thought process as we progress. It's important to share in not just African American history, but all histories that resonate and contribute to the foundation of the United States. There are many notable people who have contributed to the fabric of this country and whose achievements should be shared en masse. The calls will continue to have Confederate monuments removed and housed in museums where everyone can learn and be knowledgeable about their place in American history. Until these monuments are dismantled and rightfully stored in their appropriate place, cries will persist for equal representation and the abolishment of a celebrated and torrid past in our community neighborhoods, parks, and beyond.

MONUMENTAL ARTISTS FROM THE PAST

Art, which is the expression of creative activity and imagination usually in visual form as literature, music, painting, dance or sculpture, has always been one of the best forms of expression of thoughts. Without a doubt, it has been used to preserve history.

Art has always been created to express and communicate ideologies and to inspire to not only think, but to act as well. Before humankind learned to read, we depended solely on word of mouth or on visual symbols to express meanings and to learn something new.

Audiences to art have always varied. Art in the past had been confined to geographical location and social perceptions, and whether or not they shared values as perceived by the audience.

Today, however, with growing communication and the shrinking of the world into a global village, different levels of social diversity and literacy have caused a greater exposure of art to everyone.

Such exposure has brought more predominantly, now more than ever, the contributions of African American art to the development of culture in the United States. Up until the last century, works of black origin had not been given much attention, and its works had been drowned in its contemporary white art origin. Even worse, some were drafted into art of white background and projected as such.

The oldest images of art of black origin are said to be predated to about 24,000 to 27,000 years ago in Namibia. They were characteristically made in human-like forms. Common features of these arts included enlarged heads and hands, elongated head, pointed breasts. Other forms of art were depicted in part as animals and humans as well. These forms of art depicted power, vitality and fertility of youthfulness, and reserved demeanors of one showing a person in control.

Arts of black origin came with them a lot of storytelling. Storytelling provided not only entertainment, but also satisfied the curiosities of black people and taught important lessons about everyday life.

Traditionally, the art of black origin has had religion and culture being a great influence on it. In inception, these arts stemmed from functionalism, religious symbolism, and utilitarianism, and many art pieces created at the time were mostly used to communicate with spiritual powers, rather than for creative purposes as can be seen today.

In today's world, the art of black origin now transcends just the spiritual purposes, as we now have the visual arts of native Africa, in particular sub-Saharan Africa, with crafts such as textiles, painting, pottery, sculpture, jewelry, and decoration.

With the Middle Passage came the proliferation of the African American culture and its art. When black art crossed into the United States, it was first considered as primitive because it used different conventions in its creation when compared then to European art. It was deemed to be abstract, but this was as a result of the lack of discernment of the unique culture and traditions of the artisan of the craft.

In the early years of America, although slavery significantly restricted African Americans' ability to practice their cultural traditions, many practices, values, and beliefs survived and, over time, have modified or blended with the white culture. The result is a unique and dynamic culture that has had and continues to have a profound impact on mainstream American culture, as well as the culture of the broader world.

Over the years, the art of African American origin has greatly influenced societal changes by instilling values and translating experiences across space and time. It has served and still serves as a vehicle for social change, as it allows cultures of different origins in the United States to communicate with each other by way of images, sounds, and stories.

It has further been a renaissance for the African culture in America. It has inspired black people to establish businesses, art institutions, publishing houses, journals, and magazines. It led to the creation of African American culture programs within colleges.

Today, we see its sophistication and beauty in each detail of African American art. This has been thanks to many African American artists who have pushed arts of black origin to the forefront. These artists have spent a great deal of their lives in promoting African American art, and while they may have succeeded, little yet is known about some of these great artists.

Thankfully, today, these erroneous narratives are being corrected. Here are outstanding and ground-breaking artists past and present. Also, you will be opportune to learn the importance of public art that contributes to a community's identity, fosters community pride and a sense of belonging, and enhances the quality of life for its residents and visitors.

Augusta Savage (February 29, 1892 – March 27, 1962). Savage was considered the most leading artist of the Harlem Renaissance. As a young child, she enjoyed sculpting animals and small figures, despite her father's objection.

After winning a contest at a county fair in Florida, Savage attend The Cooper Union School of Art in New York and got a scholarship to the Fountainbleau School of the Arts in Paris.

When the selection committee found out that Savage was black, they rescinded her scholarship, fearing objection from southern white women. She took action by sending letters to the local media about the committee's discriminatory practices. Her story made headlines but did not change the committee's decision.

Savage was commissioned to create the sculpture, Harp, inspired by the words of the poem "Lift Every Voice and Sing" written by James Weldon Johnson. She also sculpted portrait bust of African American leaders such as Marcus Garvey and W.E.B. DuBois.

Savage began teaching and opened the Savage Studio of Arts and Crafts in 1932 and became the first African American artist to join the National Association of Women Painters and Sculptors.

Carroll Harris Simms (April 29, 1924–February 1, 2010). Master sculptor, ceramist, painter, jeweler, author, and educator, Carroll Harris Simms was born in Bald Knob, AR. He attended Hampton Institute of Toledo, earned his bachelor's and master's degree from the Cranbrook Academy of Art, where he was the first African American student to graduate and attended Wayne State University.

Simms joined Texas Southern University in 1950, where he taught sculpture and ceramics. During his tenure, Simms made four sculptures for the campus; The Tradition of Music, Jonah and the Whale, The Africa Queen Mother. Carroll Harris Simms Sculpture Plaza was dedicated on the campus at Texas Southern University in 1996.

His exposure to the British Museum's collection of Benin and Yoruba art influenced his sculpture and teaching methodology, and he continued his studies of West African art and culture while traveling to Nigeria on a Southern Fellowship grant in 1968. He returned to West Africa in 1973, lecturing at universities in Sierra Leone, Liberia and Nigeria. In 1977, he participated in Festac '77, a historic assembly of Pan-African artists. Simms retired from Texas Southern University in 1987.

The Carroll Harris Simms National Black Art Competition is held biannually at the African American Museum in Dallas, which has also collected his work along with TSU's University Museum; the Museum of Fine Arts, Houston; the California African American Museum in Los Angeles; and the Hampton University Museum.

Elizabeth Catlett (April 15, 1915 – April 2, 2012). Born in Washington, D.C., Catlett was raised by her grandparents. She graduated from Howard University School of Arts in 1936. She was the first African American woman to earn an MFA degree in sculpture from the University of Iowa. She moved to Illinois, where she studied ceramics at the Art Institute of Chicago and later to New York and studied lithography at the Arts Students League. Catlett's artwork depicts feminism, segregation, and the struggles of African Americans. In 1947, Catlett produced her first major show "I Am A Negro Woman."

Catlett's public art are The Invisible Man, Harlem, NY; Students Aspire, Howard University, Washington, D.C.; Louis Armstrong and Mahalia Jackson at Louis Armstrong Park, New Orleans, LA. Catlett's collection of work are held at The Art Institute of Chicago, The Museum of Modern Art in New York, the Hammer Museum in Los Angeles, and the National Gallery of Art in Washington, D.C.

James E. Lewis (August 4, 1923 – August 9, 1997). Notable sculptor and Baltimore artist, Lewis dedicated his life to creating the art department and gallery at Morgan State University, where he collected over 3,000 pieces of African American art that were dedicated to the campus art gallery.

Born in Phoenix, VA, Lewis graduated from Philadelphia College of Arts in 1942. He left college and served in the

Marines during World War II. When he returned in 1946, he graduated from Philadelphia College of Art and received his Master's degree from Temple University. Lewis was the chairman of the art department at Morgan State University for 36 years.

He raised awareness for everyone to support African American artist and collect paintings and sculptures. His public work "Black Solider" is located at the Battle Monument Plaza and Frederick Douglass at Morgan State University.

John Rhoden (March 13, 1918 – January 4, 2001) Born in Birmingham, AL, Rhoden attended Talladega College. After serving in the Army in World War II, he enrolled in the School of Painting and Sculpture at Columbia University and studied at the American Academy in Rome.

Mr. Rhoden's commissioned works include "Monumental Abstraction," on the exterior of the Metropolitan Hospital in Harlem; a nine-foot bronze sculpture of Frederick Douglass, the black abolitionist leader at Lincoln University in Pennsylvania; and "Zodiacal Structure and Curved Wall," at the Afro-American Museum in Philadelphia. The Pennsylvania Academy of Fine Arts in Philadelphia took over responsibility for more than 275 works by Rhoden.

John Wilson (1922 – January 22, 2015). Born in Roxbury, MA, sculptor, painter and printmaker, Wilson was known for his portraits of black men. He started painting and drawing at an early age and received training at the Roxbury Boys Club with Russian émigré, Alexandre Iacovleff. In 1939, he received a full scholarship at the School of the Boston Museum of Fine Arts, and graduated from Tufts University in 1947. Later, he progressed to study in Mexico City and Paris.

Wilson's involvement during the Civil Rights Movement resulted in consciously political images and using lithography to portray domestic life in the African American community to send a strong message about racial justice, income disparity, and black dignity.

Wilson created two monumental busts of Martin Luther King, Jr. for the Martin Luther King, Jr. Memorial Park in Buffalo, NY, and on permanent display in the rotunda of the U.S. Capitol Building, Washington, DC. In 1982, Wilson's monumental anonymous "head" project was commissioned for the grounds of the Museum of the National Center of African American Artists (NCAAA), later installed in 1987 and titled "Eternal Presence."

Wilson has been included in solo and group exhibitions at the University of Arizona Museum of Art (2005), Pennsylvania Academy of the Fine Arts (2014), Philadelphia Museum of Art (2015), Newark Museum (1993), Metropolitan Museum of Art (2003), Yale University Art Gallery (2011) and the Amon Carter Museum of Art (2009).

Wilson's work is in numerous prominent museum collections, including the Cleveland Art Museum, OH; deCordova Sculpture Park and Museum, Washington D.C.; Metropolitan Museum of Art, NY; Museum of Fine Arts Boston, MA; Museum of Modern Art, NY; Museum of the National Center of Afro-American Artists, Washington D.C.; National Portrait Gallery, Washington D.C.; Philadelphia Museum of Art, PA; Rose Art Museum, Brandeis University, MA; Smith College Museum of Art, MA; Tufts University Art Galleries, MA; University of Arizona Museum of Art, AZ and the University of Wisconsin's collection, WI.

Meta Vaux Warrick Fuller (June 9, 1877 – March 18, 1968). Meta Vaux Warrick Fuller career as an artist spanned for over seventy years. She was the first African American woman artist to receive a commission from the U.S. government. Her art reflected African American historical events. In high school, her project was chosen to be included in the 1893 World's Columbian Exposition and she won a scholarship to the Pennsylvania Museum & School of Industrial Art.

After her graduation, Fuller traveled to Paris to become the protégé of sculptor Auguste Rodin, where she had her work displayed in several galleries.

In 1902, Fuller returned to Philadelphia and continued creating signatures pieces such as Ethiopia Awakening, which is considered to be the first Pan-African American work of art.

She created the Emancipation statue in 1913 to commemorate the 50th anniversary of the Emancipation Proclamation. In 1999, precisely 86 years later, the statue was cast in bronze and is located in the Harriet Tubman Square in Boston, MA.

Michael Rolando Richards (August 2, 1963–September 11, 2001). Tragically perished by a terrorist attack, in his art studio on the 92nd floor in the World Trade Center on 9/11. Richards, a talented sculptor, was born in Brooklyn, NY. He received his Master of Arts degree from New York University. Richards was influenced by the Black Arts Movement.

In one of his numerous works, Richards wrote that his art allows for an examination of the psychic conflict which results from the desire to both belong to and resist a society which denies blackness even as it affirms. He said, "In attempting to make this pain and alienation concrete, I use my body, the primary locus of experience as a die from which to make casts. These function as surrogates and as an entry into the work."

Richards' art addressed social injustice and oppression of the African American community. His well-known statues are "Are You Down" located at the Franconia Sculpture Park in Franconia, MN and Tar Baby vs. Sebastian located at the North Carolina Museum of History. Both statues depict the legacy of the Tuskegee Airmen.

Oliver LaGrone (December 9, 1906 – October 15, 1995). LaGrone was a sculptor, humanitarian, poet and educator.

Born in McAlester, OK, LaGrone was the first African American student at Cranbrook Academy of Art and graduated from the University of New Mexico in 1938 with a Bachelor's degree in Fine Arts and Sociology. He wrote his first poetry book entitled, "Footfalls: Poetry from America's Becoming" in 1949. LaGrone had poems and reviews published in the Negro Digest and the New York Times Sunday Book Review.

On May 1976, LaGrone created two statues, "The University of Family" and "The Dancer" located on the campus of Penn State Worthington Scranton campus. February 3, 1980 and 1993 was proclaimed Oliver LaGrone Day in Harrisburg, PA, for his contributions to the community.

Richmond Barthé (January 28, 1901 – March 5, 1989). Harlem Renaissance sculptor, Richmond Barthé, was born in Bay St. Louis, MS. From 1924 to 1928, Barthé attended and studied painting at the Art Institute of Chicago. Even though he mainly studied painting, Barthé's talent as a sculptor was recognized by his fellow students and local critics in Chicago. In 1928, he put on a one-man show that was sponsored by the Chicago Women's Club.

He turned to sculpture early in his career, some of which was commissioned as public art. He sculpted an American eagle for the Social Security Building in Washington, D.C. and a bas-relief for the Harlem River Housing Project. In 1949, the Haitian government commissioned him to create monuments to the revolutionary leaders, Toussaint L'Overture and Jean Jacques Dessalines, in Port-au-Prince. In addition to spending time in Haiti, Barthé lived in Jamaica before returning to the United States and settling in southern California.

During his sixty-year career, Barthé received numerous awards for his art, including the Rosenwald Fellowship and the Guggenheim Fellowship.

Selma Burke (December 31, 1900 – August 29, 1995). Selma Burke was born in Mooresville, NC. She received her formal educational training from Winston Salem University and graduated from St. Agnes Training School for Nurses as a registered nurse in 1924.

In 1940, Burke opened the Selma Burke School of Sculpture in New York City, and graduated with a Master of Fine Arts from Columbia University in 1941. She was one of the first African American women to enroll in the Navy in 1942. While in the Navy, Burke was commissioned to do a bronze bas-relief portrait of President Franklin Delano Roosevelt, which is currently the United States dime.

Burke's public art of Martin Luther King, Jr., is at Marshall Park in Charlotte, NC that was her last public artwork.

Tina Allen (December 9, 1949 – September 9, 2008). Born in Hempstead, NY, artist and social activist, Tina Allen began painting at the age of five. She was discovered at the age of 10 by William Zorach, who was considered one of the greatest living sculptors in the world. Her first bust was a three-dimensional bust of Aristotle in high school.

Allen received her Bachelor's degree in fine arts in 1978 from the University of Southern Alabama. She then moved to New York City and attended the New York School of Visual Arts and received her Master's degree from Pratt Institute. In 1986, Allen won the commission to create a memorial statue in Boston, MA, of labor activist and organizer of Brotherhood of Sleeping Car Porters, A. Philip Randolph. She won the contest and her career took off.

Allen's public works include Celes King, Jr., Alex Haley, Martin Luther King, Jr., Sojourner Truth, and Tupac Shakur (that has been removed in Stone Mountain, GA, in 2015).

CONVERSATION CORNER WITH ARTISTS

"Public art is a reflection of the values of a community."

- Vinnie Bagwell

ANTHONY PEYTON PORTER

Author Anthony Peyton Porter (Photo courtesy of Anthony Peyton Porter).

Anthony Peyton Porter, a native Chicagoan, is the author of seven books, including *Jump at de Sun: The Story of Zora Neale Hurston, Can He Say That?* and *Zina Garrison: Ace.* He has served as president of the boards of Alchemy Theatre, SASE: The Write Place, and the Minnesota Center for Arts Criticism.

Porter collaborated on The Clayton-Jackson-McGhie Memorial in Duluth, Minn. In June 1920, three black men—Elias Clayton, Elmer Jackson, and Isaac McGhie, were wrongly accused of raping a white woman. Porter chose the fourteen quotes on the walls, including the words of Euripides, Elie Wiesel, James Baldwin, Siddhartha Gautama, and Anne Lamott. The L-shaped monument was dedicated on October 10, 2003.

Tammy Gibson: Mr. Porter, what is your background?
Anthony Porter: I'm a writer and I've been an editor since the 1980s. I started out writing for children because I wanted to change the world. For the past five years, I've taught creative writing at High Desert State Prison in Susanville, California.

TG: How did you get involved in the Duluth memorial?
AP: In the late 1990s, a small group formed a committee to raise money to commemorate the victims of a public murder in Duluth, Minnesota in June 1920. Carla Stetson, a sculptor, went to college with my wife and lived in Duluth. Carla wanted to submit a proposal because she knew my work, and asked me to collaborate with her. My being the American Negro she knew probably didn't hurt.

Carla and I agreed on an approach for the project, submitted our proposal to the committee, and we were selected. Carla designed the memorial and created the sculptures, and I chose the quotes and wrote the summary on the wall next to the figures of Clayton, Jackson, and McGhie.

Clayton Jackson McGhie Memorial in Duluth, MN.

TG: This year marks the 100th anniversary of the Duluth lynching of Elias Clayton, Elmer Jackson, and Isaac McGhie in 1920. Did you know about the tragedy before being selected?
AP: No, I hadn't heard about the lynchings, so I read a book written by Michael Fedo entitled *The Lynchings in Duluth*, based on oral accounts and newspaper articles about the killings. He wrote the book so people would know what had occurred. Fedo's book was my primary source.

TG: What was your reaction at the unveiling of the Duluth memorial.
AP: I loved it. There were hundreds of people there, and it was extremely satisfying. I smiled nonstop. The dedication confirmed for me that the two years it had taken us, mostly Carla, had been well spent. From my finding of Michael Fedo's book to the hours at the library, I learned a lot and I'm glad I got to do it.

TG: It must be gratifying to know that your quotes will be a part of the memorial for many years?
AP: Absolutely. It's the only time my words have been cast in bronze. It's not likely to happen again, and it's very satisfying as a writer. To think that at the intersection of First Street and Second Avenue in Duluth, my grandchildren could say "My grandfather did that" is irresistible.

TG: What projects are you currently working on?
AP: I'm morphing into a poet. I wrote six nonfiction books in the early nineties, and for nine years, I wrote a newspaper column in Chico [California]. Now I'm trying to learn how to write poetry. I don't have a specific goal in mind, but I'm looking forward to wherever I'm headed. Most of my time is devoted to figuring out how to teach writing to my 43 students in prison.

TG: What advice do you have for an aspiring poet?
AP: Read as much good writing as you can and practice writing, not just thinking about it, but actually writing. I didn't get up the gumption to think of myself as a writer until I was over thirty. I wasted precious time. I wrote for 12 years before my first book.

Writing doesn't require much equipment. Anybody who wants to write can write. Nobody has to see it.

DEBRA HAND

Artist Debra Hand standing next to the statue of Paul Laurence Dunbar.
(Photo courtesy of Debra Hand Studios)

Self-taught artist and sculptor, Debra Hand was discovered by artist and founder of the DuSable Museum, Dr. Margaret Burroughs. Hand's work is featured at the DuSable Museum, United Negro College Fund Collection, and the Smithsonian Institution Anacostia Museum. The Chicago Park District and Dunbar Advisory Council commissioned Hand to create the nine-foot tall statue of poet Paul Laurence Dunbar located on the southside of Chicago. Hand has received numerous honors for her outstanding work.

Tammy Gibson: Can you tell me your background and what inspired you to be a sculptor?
Debra Hand: I was born and raised in Chicago, and my education culminated with a Master's Degree in Information Technology from Northwestern University McCormick School of Engineering in Evanston, IL.

TG: What was your experience working with Dr. Margaret Burrough? What did you learn from her?
DH: I never had a working relationship with Dr. Burroughs, rather it was a relationship that formed into a mother/daughter bond. She discovered my work and introduced me to the art world. She first looked at my work when I was a painter. Later, when I began sculpting, she was excited about my potential and asked me to create a piece for the DuSable Museum. She instructed that I present that piece to her on the DuSable stage during the opening of the Dr. Margaret Burroughs' retrospective exhibit titled "Lifetime in the Arts." She then arranged for me to be included in my first public exhibition at the South Shore Cultural Center. In our relationship, we always spoke about using culture to help our communities and to give back to mankind at large. Dr. Burroughs left clear examples for everyone to learn from through her founding of such institutions as the founder of the DuSable Museum, the South Side Community Arts Center, and the South Shore Cultural Center Gallery. Dr. Burroughs was a very loving person with a gentle spirit, but she was powerful in her convictions and mighty in her ability to see a vision and carry it out.

TG: What artist inspired you?
DH: Dr. Burroughs is my greatest inspiration. I am also inspired by sculptor Richard Hunt, and by the painter/sculptor, Pablo Picasso.

TG: What was your first sculpture?
DH: I have no photos of it, but it was a sculpture I created from looking at a tree branch, which reminded me of an abstract warrior.

TG: How would you define yourself as an artist?
DH: I am a self-taught artist and writer who is using art as an end to the means. My end goal is to be a blessing to humankind in some way through my work.

Paul Laurence Dunbar Statue at Dunbar Park in Chicago, IL.
(Photo courtesy of Debra Hand Studios)

TG: What is your favorite sculpture you created and why?
DH: My favorite sculpture is the Paul Dunbar statue I created. I have always admired his work as a writer. His poems were read to me as a child.

TG: What are the steps in designing a statue?
DH: The answer depends on the project. If someone has hired me to honor someone's life, I first start with researching the person and their legacy. Then, I brainstorm ideas on how I might symbolize the theme of their life and embody it in a work of art. I also begin to think about the materials that are best suited for the project. Finally, I begin the work in whatever material I've chosen.

TG: What materials do you use to make your statues?
DH: Depending on the piece, I use copper, wood, bronze, clay, resin, epoxy, and sometimes, pieces from found objects.

TG: What is the best material for outdoor statues and what tools do you use?
DH: Bronze or other metals. I use standard tools... among them are electric tools, saws, drills, and carving tools.

TG: How did you feel when you were selected you to sculpt Paul Laurence Dunbar statue?
DH: I was very honored to have the opportunity to encapsulate Dunbar's legacy within a work of art for my hometown.

TG: What material was used to design the Paul Laurence Dunbar statue and the size and weight?
DH: The statue is made of bronze. The Dunbar statue is 6ft. tall (excluding the solid granite base) and the statue alone weighs 500 to 600 lbs. It took between a year and 18 months to finalize everything, including the installation. There are many additional steps when creating a public sculpture, which includes working with an architect and engineer to design a foundation that has to support such great weight;

working with a construction crew to excavate the site and pour the concrete foundation; working with granite cutter to cut the stone for the granite base; making the original life-size model and making a mold of it to create a wax model. Working with the foundry to pour the bronze, and overseeing the installation of the granite and the statue on the site.

TG: What projects are you working on now?
DH: I am currently more focused on content creation and writing for the online magazine, Black Art in America.

TG: What advice do you have for young women who want to be a sculptor?
DH: Just start somewhere like I did. I became a sculptor after helping my son with a school project that required me to buy some clay. That was how it all started. I picked up some clay and just formed whatever came out of my hands. It doesn't matter if it's a masterpiece. It matters that they start the process of sculpting. This is the crucial step. Start. Once they pick up some clay, they will be led through the steps of getting better, just by sheer passion alone. They will begin to look for things to try next and for more information on processes. They have the advantage of online videos to teach them things it took me many years to learn on my own through trial and error. Just start! Go to the local hobby store and buy some clay that will air dry. That way, they won't need any special equipment but their hands to step into a new world of creativity.

FREDERICK HIGHTOWER

Artist Frederick Hightower standing next to the
statue of Katherine Johnson.

Frederick Hightower is a visionary fine artist who provides an invaluable, unique, custom service that infuses his inspired creative portraits and artwork. The style he uses in his artwork is a centuries-old classical technique inspired by Flemish Realism and developed by such artists as Vermeer and Rebens of the 16th and 17th centuries respectively.

His ability to express and manifest the heart of a concept through visual art is a gift that captures what words cannot. He works with people intuitively to help bring those challenging ideas to fruition, usually in a way that speaks the essence of the idea more clearly and with visionary creativity.

Frederick Hightower's portraits and sculptures are beautifully crafted museum quality that captures the character of the person in a classical realist style.

TG: Can you tell me your background and what inspired you to be a sculptor?
FH: I was born in a coal-mining town in Madison, West Virginia. At a young age, my family moved to Charlottesville, VA, for a few years and came back to West Virginia. I graduated with a degree in Fine Arts at West Virginia State University. I'm also a pastor and very involved in the ministry. I have been doing artwork all my life since I was a child. I have painted more than I have sculpted. I've done small sculptures, but getting the opportunity to do a large monument was breaking into the big leagues for an artist. Katherine Johnson was my first major sculpture and I'm working on another one right now, so I'm looking forward to future commissions.

TG: Regarding the Robert E. Lee statue in Charlottesville, VA, where you once lived, how do feel about Confederate monuments in public places, especially in African American communities?
FH: I'm more interested in producing African American monuments. On a gut level, I'm very opposed to racism. Growing up in Charlottesville, VA, I did face racism.

Personally, with the senseless murder of George Floyd, the pandemic of racism, discrimination, and police brutality, all confederate monuments should be removed and be replaced with statues honoring African Americans, provided that African American sculptors are commissioned to create them. Many of the African American statues are not created by African American artist. To me, that's a hidden form of racism. The Board tends to choose Caucasian sculptors, and oftentimes, African American sculptors are excluded. African American statues are those that are not just of African American but those that are created by African Americans. There is a push back against African Americans creating our own statues because there is a lot of money in it. We really have to fight to do our own statues and a lot of people don't recognize that. Sometimes our worst enemies are our own people because, we as a people, think that white ice is better than black ice.

There was opposition for me as an African American to produce Katherine Johnson's statue. This is because they felt that I didn't matriculate from the right school even though I graduated from West Virginia State University, the same college Katherine Johnson graduated in 1937. They wanted someone with a big name and had a big resume and credentials. Usually, that takes out the majority of African American sculptors. If African American statues are going up, they could at least look for African American sculptors. When Caucasian statues are being designed, trust me, 90% of the sculptors are Caucasians. When bids come up to do Native American statues, they will only need Native Americans to apply.

I believe in Black History. I want to see our sculptures go up and see our people being celebrated. But I would also like to be part of the process of helping to make that happen. The only way that can happen is when the Committees come up to do a sculpture that they bring to the table to first seek an African American sculptor.

TG: What artists inspired you?

FH: I have been inspired by the realism of Nigerian sculptors. The sculptures and head bust bear no names of the artists. Many are in the British museum from the European colonization. They found these sculptures and head bust, and they were shocked because they didn't believe that they were designed by black artists. I believe the reason why I'm an artist is because I had an ancestor that did this hundreds of years ago. Art runs in my family. One of my great grandfathers, who was a mason, designed the marvel work that was done for the Capitol in Washington, DC and built the Greenbriar Hotel in White Sulphur Springs, WV. I have also been inspired by the work of European sculptors such as Michelangelo's Pieta and David.

Bronze statue of Katherine Johnson at
West Virginia State University.

TG: How did you feel when you were commissioned to do the Katherine Johnson statue?

FH: I was originally commissioned to do a bust of Katherine Johnson. A lady came to me and told me that I needed to do her friend, Katherine Johnson's statue. I didn't know about Ms. Johnson, so I watched the movie "Hidden Figures." I created a prototype, presented it to West Virginia State University and it was President Anthony Jenkins, who selected me to do the statue. The bronze statue weighs around 1,500 pounds and it took me five months to complete the project.

TG: How did you feel the day of the dedication and unveiling of Katherine Johnson's statue?

FH: I was excited and it was wonderful to honor Katherine Johnson. The unveiling was more about her than the sculpture. Here is a woman whose 100 years of life was a wonderful testimony. If you strive for excellence, a person of good character, integrity and you perfect the gift that God gave you, which she did, in the end, you will be recognized. It was a wonderful tribute, not just about the sculpture, but all the people who came to celebrate her. For our little school, West Virginia State University, that was the biggest event the college has ever had. They weren't expecting such a large turnout. So, I am honored and thankful that I was allowed to play a small part in recognizing such a great woman like Katherine Johnson. It was one of the highlights of my life.

TG: What current project are you working on?

FH: I'm working on a basketball statue of Hal Greer, one of the first basketball players to go into the NBA and the first African American athlete to receive a scholarship at Marshall University. It will be a 12-foot statue of Greer doing a jump shot.

TG: What advice would you give to an aspiring sculptor?

FH: Work on your craft, perfect it, promote yourself, strive for excellence, and be the best you can be.

GEORGE NOCK

Artist George Nock standing next to "The Gift" statue.
(Photo courtesy of George Nock)

Former running back with the New York Jets and Washington Redskins, George Nock, was destined early in life to become an artist. With a fascinating career – from maneuvering his powerful torso, swift moves on the Gridiron, positioning his big, strong hands to mold objects of intricacy and perfection delicately. Nock has distinguished himself among the greatest sculptors of the twentieth through the twenty-first century due to an intrinsic ability to capture with versatility highly original bronzes, reflecting life's experiences. The brawny, broad-shouldered ex-athlete found his real victory in shaping exquisite sculpture. A proud alumnus of Morgan State College, now, Morgan State University, Nock designed the statues of two icon coaches, Edward P. Hurt and Earl C. Banks at the university's Legend's Plaza.

Tammy Gibson: Mr. Nock, can you tell me your background an amazing career?
George Nock: I grew up in Philadelphia, and I was first introduced to clay at the age of seven in the second grade. I picked up the clay, sculpted it, and I realized I could make a horse from it.

It was kind of proportional because it had a beautiful big body and skinny legs, but the clay fell. It was an oil-based clay. I was a little upset, but I asked myself what animal had strong legs and could withstand their weight. So, I designed a dinosaur. All the kids in my class wanted me to make a dinosaur for them. So, that whole afternoon, I was dedicated to making things out of clay.

After a while, my mom saw that I was not going to stop drawing, so she helped by getting art materials because I was messing up all of her books. When I attended junior high school, I met two teachers, one was a sculptor and the other was a painter. They saw my talent and gave me the opportunity to exhibit my talent. They would take me out of some of my classes to come to their class to work and practice. I thought they would bring me in to teach and guide me to be a sculptor, but instead, both of them let me work on my artwork the way I wanted to and at my own pace.

It served me well because it was all my creativity, utilizing and learning the materials that kept me on the straight and narrow, as far as being interested and continuing to ask questions of "What if I did this?" "What if I did that."

I was asked to do an 8ft x10ft mural for a project when I was in junior high school. I did all the drawings, the deadline was coming, and I needed help with my project. As a result, we finished the mural on time, but the two people that helped me complete the project got as much billing for it as I did. I said to myself, "How can that be? Hey, it is what it is?" I can't remember what the picture was about, but it was impressive, and I was wondering what was going to happen to it because they did it on thick paper and not on a canvas.

One teacher asked me to come to an art class he had every Saturday in south Philadelphia. I volunteered because it was doing something I wanted to do. I would sculpt anything that came to mind, primarily animals.

During my high school years, I progressed in how I utilized the material. I still have three pieces from that era. It was remarkable that I still had good form, but that helped me graduate to the next level in art. It also helped me become critical of my own work as well, trying to develop my craft as I went up the ladder to become an artist.

I was heavenly involved in sports. I played basketball, football, and track. I earned a scholarship from Morgan State College and I also earned a scholarship to Tulsa University.

Back then, you had to submit your photo with the application to be enrolled in the program. Prior to submitting my application, the coach from Tulsa University would call me every week to say, "I can't wait to get you down here." After I sent the application with my photo, I never heard from him again. I realized that was not the university to attend. As a result, I went to Morgan State College. I played football but I didn't take any art classes, except for the ones that were mandatory for me to graduate. I discontinued taking drawing and painting classes on my own because it was too constrictive. I had to do it their way and it wasn't fitting my needs. I would still go to the art classes to visit because I had friends who were artists and I would occasionally draw with them. The development was still there, so I knew that as long as I continued to draw, I would develop my style and approach to creating work on my own.

TG: How long did you play professional football?
GN: I played for the NFL for five years. I was a running back for three seasons with the New York Jets and two seasons with the Washington Redskins.

During my third season playing for the New York Jets, I had a friend who was a quarterback. He had put together an art group that would have art shows around the east coast. He invited me to one of his shows. This was after I retired from football because I tore my knee up when I played for the Washington Redskins and I was never able to recover properly to play the position of running back. The injury altered my style of running.

TG: Was it challenging to transition from being a professional football player to a sculptor?
GN: No, I was doing artwork before I became a football player. While in the hospital when I tore up my knee, I would go through a lot of things, especially as I was immobile. and wondering "what am I going to do now?" With a degree in psychology, I knew I could get a job in social services. During the football off-season in New York, I worked at a Montessori school system program as a troubleshooter. When there were in-house problems with teachers, administrators, and students, I was there to calm any situations.

After I retired, I lived in Reston, VA. I got a job in community services working with at-risk children who had behavioral and drug problems, and I helped to give them some guidance.

TG: How were you commissioned to design the statues of legendary coaches Edward P. Hurt and Earl C. Banks at Morgan State University?
GN: In 1966, Morgan State College Bears played in the Tangerine Bowl, which is now called the Citrus Bowl. We played against West Chester Rams, an all-white college and beat them 14-6. We beat them in such a way that by the end of the first half, we had more penalty yardage than we had regular yards. It was evident that they were trying to keep the score down. There was no chance West Chester was going to win. It was the first time an HBCU or University won an integrated football bowl game.

On the 50th anniversary of the 1966 Citrus Bowl, I was one of ten players and their wives who were invited to the New Year's Day game at the Citrus Bowl in Orlando, FL. We received a standing ovation and accolades for winning the 1966 Tangerine Citrus Bowl.

Statues of Coach Edward P. ("Eddie") Hurt and Coach Earl C. ("Papa Bear") Banks at Morgan State University's Legends Plaza.

At the game, I met a few people, including Dr. David Wilson, President of Morgan State University, who were working on projects on how to honor individuals from the past who made contributions to Morgan State. If you look at both coaches' records, Coach Hurt won championships in track and field, basketball, and football. He had a winning streak in football with 54 straight wins. Coach Banks had a 31-football game winning streak when I played for him. Many college teams did not want to play against us and they kept dropping us because they knew they were going to lose. By the time I arrived at Morgan State College, the football team only played eight games a year.

I talked with Dr. Wilson, President at Morgan State University, and he asked me to look around the campus and see what I wanted to do to commemorate Coaches Hurt and Banks. Dr. Wilson wanted to name the area on campus, The Legends Plaza, where we can honor other legends as well.

I stayed a few days at Morgan State University walking around the campus, taking photographs. I found a location, did the layout and design for The Legends Plaza. I presented it to Dr. Wilson and started working on the statues. I knew my feet were under the fire because I had to make sure the statues look just like the coaches. When I'm commissioned to do a project, I always do a two-foot model to let people see how the sculpture is going to look. I had to show the maquette to the families of Coach Banks and Coach Hurt for their approval.

At the presentation, Coach Banks' wife said the model looked perfect and the only thing I didn't do well enough was the fact that he was more pigeon-toed and would sometimes put one foot on top of the other. I had made the model of Coach Banks slightly pigeon-toed. Mrs. Banks said, "You know he was more pigeon-toed than that." Therefore, I made sure to make the change. The granddaughter of Coach Hurt cried and said the statue looked just like her grandfather. After getting positive feedback from the family members and team players, I knew I was on the right track.

TG: What was your inspiration for designing the statues of Coaches Hurt and Banks?
GN: I knew Coach Hurt and I played for Coach Banks as well. They both had amazing careers. Every student that attends Morgan State University needs to know how great these men were and how they made an impact at the university, especially when it came to sports.

TG: How long did it take you to design the statues?
GN: It took me seven months to complete both statues. I don't know how I did it, but it came to fruition. Every day was a grind to finish the statues by the deadline.

TG: How did you feel when the statues were unveiled at the dedication?
GN: I was happy and elated. At first, I didn't think anyone knew about the unveiling. So many people came to the dedication that no one could not find parking. There were hundreds of people, and it seemed like they came out of nowhere, which made me feel good. The most rewarding comment I heard about the statues was, "It looks just like him."

TG: As an African American artist, do find it challenging to get commission work to design statues?
GN: Absolutely. The thing is, whenever people have in mind of doing something substantial and paying decent money for statues, they tend to think that African Americans are not on par. But we are more on par with the sculptures because we know we have a reputation that we have to defend, and it has to be supported by the work that we do.

I've had people come to me and ask me about doing pieces. I give them a price; they go back and look at other websites and end up going to a white person. I've missed so many opportunities because they didn't think I can do statues of Caucasians. However, I can do a Caucasian statue just as well, if not better, than most.

TG: What project are you most proud of in your career?
GN: The Morgan State project is what I'm most proud of. As a graduate of the university, it was very personal and a way of letting the school and country know how good these two coaches were.

Another project that I'm proud of is the Milty's Realm statue at the Milton Library in Milton, GA.

Milty's Realm statue at the Milton Library in Milton GA. (Photo courtesy of George Nock)

Currently, I'm working on a statue of two little league baseball players, one black, one white, and they met at the Florida Little League State Championship Tournament in Orlando, FL. In August 1955, the all-black Pensacola Jaycees played against the all-white Orlando Kiwanis. It was the areas first racially integrated Little League Championship baseball game in the South. The statues will be installed at the Lorna Doone Park in Orlando, FL later this year.

TG: What is the best advice do you have an aspiring artist?
GN: You have to do your homework to make what you do better than you did before. With each piece that you do, you grow. The objective is to be better than you were yesterday. You will see the development of your work become much more pleasing to you, and that's the first person that has to critique it.

NIJEL BINNS

Artist Nijel Binns standing next to the Mother of Humanity®
Monument in Watts, CA. (Photo courtesy of Nijel Binns)

Nijel Binns is accomplished in portrait sculpture and painting in the realist tradition. His artistic expression also includes three published books on the martial arts, a Screen Actors Guild/AFTRA membership for stunt work, and a motion picture fight choreographer of five films.

Tammy Gibson: What is your background and primary influence of becoming a sculptor?
Nijel Binns: I was born in England, raised in Jamaica, and moved with my family to Newark, New Jersey.

For four years, I went to the United States Air Force. After leaving the military, I got involved in martial arts films. I was a stuntman in "The Big Brawl", Jackie Chan's first film in 1980. I worked on a couple of films such as the original Karate Kid II with actor Ralph Macchio and doing some fight coordinating. On my off time, I started working to develop my fine art interests, and that's what led me to a career in sculpting.

TG: What artists or professionals have inspired you to do art?
NB: I took a trip back to England in 1972, where I saw the "Treasures of Tutankhamun" exhibit at the British Museum. It was from that moment that I got inspired by art.

Some of the things I saw at the museum where stemming back to our old traditions in Ancient Kemet and realizing that we were able to achieve such artistic brilliance just blew my mind. In terms of people who were inspirational in my life, it was Michael Jackson and the Jackson family, particularly Michael. I was very inspired by his life from the first time I saw him on the Ed Sullivan show and up to the chance of working with him and being his bodyguard. Another person that inspired me more when I got out of the military and moved to Los Angeles was Paul Robeson. He was pivotal, a man of many disciplines. He was a singer, actor, athlete, and activist. At that point, I realized that I don't have to be stuck just doing one thing. Paul Robeson definitely proved that you can have excellence in all of those fields.

TG: What was your first art job?
NB: My first professional sculpting job was to create the "Top Selling Artist of the Decade Award" in 1990. It was created for Michael Jackson on behalf of his record company, CBS Epic, now Sony Records.

TG: You were also commissioned by the Michael Jackson Fan Club to create a bas-relief award on behalf of the fans worldwide. What was that experience creating the award and meeting Michael Jackson?
NB: I met Michael Jackson before being commissioned to create "The Michael Jackson 30th Anniversary Fan Award" in 2002. I was at home watching television and seeing Michael accepting the "Top Selling Artist of the Decade Award" I created for him in 1990. I was so new to the business, and later realized I should have negotiated to be there when the award was being presented. I made sure I called his record company, MJJ Productions and told them I was the guy that created the award and asked if Michael can send me an autograph picture. When I received the picture in 1990, Michael signed his photo and wrote the date 1998 and put three circles underneath the date and an arrow. I didn't know what it meant, but I was appreciative.

Fast forward, to the year 1998, I was doing security at Universal Studios. My supervisor came up to me and said that I have to escort someone really special through the "Alien Encounter" maze at Universal Studios during Halloween Horror Nights. I'm standing there and guess who popped up? It was Michael Jackson and his two children! When I met Michael, there was an extraordinarily strong spiritual energy that let me know I was in the presence of somebody very special.

The photograph he sent me in 1990 was prophetic. He wrote the year of 1998 with three circles and an arrow underneath it is going up. The interpretation we met on October 31, 1998, three months before the year was up. When I was commissioned years later to do The Michael Jackson 30th Anniversary Fan Award, that was my second time meeting him.

"The Top Selling Artist of the Decade Award"
for Michael Jackson designed by artist Nijel Binns.
(Photo courtesy of Nijel Binns)

TG: I'm sure Michael Jackson loved the bas-relief award?

NB: Yes, he did. I actually created three sculptures of him, which he kept at his Neverland Ranch. The first piece that was given to his father, Joe Jackson, in 1985 was a ceramic gold plated bust of Michael wearing his iconic aviator glasses. The second piece that Michael was extremely happy with was the Top Selling Artist of the Decade Award I created in 1990. The third piece that I was commissioned to create was a bas-relief award on behalf of his fans worldwide. Michael loved his fans very much, so that award was very special to him.

TG: Which public art project are you most proud of?
NB: I am most proud of my Mother of Humanity® Monument in Watts, California. The monument was unveiled on Mother's Day, May 11, 1996. It's the first monument ever in the history of humankind to acknowledge the African woman as the Mother of All Humanity. It is one of the largest bronze monuments in California. It is rare that an artist can do something unprecedented, and that is what the Mother of Humanity® is. Nowhere in history has any recognition been given to the black woman for being the mother of all civilization. It has never happened before. The Mother of Humanity® monument was one of those creations that has awakened our realization that we are one human family with one common future. It has had a significant impact on human consciousness.

She is standing 16 feet tall on a globe of the Earth with her left foot forward and holding a feather of peace and truth in the right hand. It's a very symbolic work of art.

I am most pleased that in 2002, I was commissioned to create the only statue of the famous American child actress, Shirley Temple. She was in attendance for the unveiling of the life-sized bronze statue at the 20th Century Fox Studio lot. It is ironic because as a child star, when Shirley Temple performed with tap dancer Bill "Bojangles" Robinson, in one of her most memorable films, The Little Colonel in 1935, they held hands dancing down the stairs together. That scene had to be cut out of the film because they couldn't show a black man holding the hands of a white woman or child. Decades later, the hands of a black man created the only statue of Shirley Temple in existence. The universe has a way of correcting things.

Artist Nijel Binns standing next to the late actress Shirley Temple and statue. (Photo courtesy of Nijel Binns)

TG: The original Tupac Shakur statue in Stone Mountain, GA, was removed in 2015. A new statue is in the works, and you were commissioned to immortalize the West Coast rapper. What is the status of the completion of the statue?
NB: Real estate developer, Jim Burnett, was in communication with Tupac's mother, Afeni Shakur. He made a promise to her to keep Tupac's memory alive. A childhood friend that lives in Atlanta and knows my body of work put me in touch with Mr. Burnett, and I got the commission to create the statue that was supposed to be installed at the Tupac Shakur Center for the Performing Arts in Stone Mountain, GA. Unfortunately, the property was sold; however, we are looking at establishing the statue in Los Angeles. It will be more relevant because Tupac had history in Los Angeles and Oakland. The location where the Mother of Humanity® statue is located is where the Tupac statue will be installed.

I am in communication with the Estate of Tupac Shakur, but nothing can be done until after the pandemic.

TG: Do you have any advice for aspiring artists?
NB: I would like aspiring artists to know that there is hardly anything new that hasn't already been done. If you go within and study yourself first, make your life the highest expression of a work of art that you can create. Then whatever comes from you, will live up to who you are.

SHELEEN P. JONES

Artist Sheleen P. Jones
(Photo courtesy of Sheleen P. Jones)

Sheleen P. Jones is an artist whose sculptures can be seen throughout New Orleans. Her art reflects life and pays homage to African Americans who have shaped and contributed to the achievements of The Crescent City's civil rights and musical influences. Jones' mission is to capture images through her sculptures, to celebrate the strength, humanity, and beauty of her vibrant community.

Tammy Gibson: Sheleen, can you discuss your background?
Sheleen Jones: I was born in what is now called the Big Easy. I studied drafting, woodworking, and general art classes that the public schools of New Orleans had offered, which gave me informed directions toward being a visual artist. I began my studies at Xavier University of Louisiana, receiving a Bachelor's degree in Fine Arts and Florida State University with a Master's degree in Fine Arts with a concentration in Sculpture.

TG: How do you describe your style of work?
SJ: Most of my public work is figurative. It pays homage to people who led the way for civil rights and regulations. I created memorial pieces such as A.P. Tureaud Sr., the civil rights attorney for the New Orleans chapter of the NAACP, who believed in taking the fight to the courthouse, and Reverend Avery C. Alexander, a civil rights activist who was elected to the Louisiana House of Representatives as a Democrat, who led many protestors up and down the streets demanding equality for African Americans.

TG: How do you seek opportunities as an artist?
SJ: I'm an optimist, who always move in the path of exciting opportunities. When someone knocks on your door, you can only hear what you are prepared for. I prepared myself to be open and ready to have opportunities come my way. While working at Southern University, I was asked to put my name on the list to create the A.P. Tureaud Sr. sculpture. My first thought was, "I don't create those types of sculptures and

I've never used that level of detail on my work." But then I realized that wasn't my voice saying that, but fear. My true voice was, "If an opportunity comes your way, you have to seek it." I changed my mind and put my name on the list.

I started collecting my figurative work that clearly demonstrated the level of detail that I can work on to present to the committee members. From that, I received the commission to do the A.P. Tureaud Sr. sculpture. The sculpture was installed in 1997 and a few years later, a pastor saw my name at the bottom of the statue and called me to create another sculpture. A lot of opportunities were words of mouth and looking at the work I created.

Marching Brass Band Sculpture at Louis Armstrong Park in New Orleans, LA.

TG: How were you selected to design the New Orleans Marching Brass Band and "Big Chief Tootie" Montana statues?

SJ: I was selected based on previous work experience. My experience gave me the ability to maintain a timely schedule, quality work, and known resources to complete the job for the outgoing mayor administration's vision for the Louis Armstrong Park.

TG: How did you feel when the statues were unveiled?

SJ: I was proud to have my pieces at Armstrong Park in New Orleans. The joy and pride people felt was overwhelming. The organizations these sculptures represented were a great sign of respect to their life-long crafts. One artist I admire is Elizabeth Catlett. She has two sculptures in the Sculpture Garden. She was 93 years old and in attendance for the opening. It was an honor to be alongside her at the unveiling.

TG: What do you dislike about the art world?

SJ: My only challenge is that figurative artists are becoming a rarity. The artist who can create actual people are moving more toward abstract pieces of work. I appreciate abstract work, but I rarely create it for myself. Usually, the work I engage in has physical features. Figurative work is unique, and few people can create it, so it's becoming a rarity.

TG: How do you feel about the misrepresentation of African American sculptors, especially women, who are not getting commission work to do African American statues?

SJ: I believe that artists were not given the opportunity and recognition due to segregation and racist practices in the past, and unfortunately, it is still relevant today. Now that we have access to information, it's easier to get commission work. For African American women, we weren't taken seriously because it's a man's vision of the world we were living in. Through the persistence of so many people, women and men, we are slowly getting respect as artists and sculptors, but we still have a long way to go because we are still working for representation.

TG: How does your family feel about your public work displayed in New Orleans? I know they are proud of you?
SJ: My family is very proud of my work. It is nice when my family comes to visit and I show them the different sculptures around the city that I created. But overall, they are proud.

TG: Are there any future artists in the family?
SJ: No, future sculptors as of yet, but my daughter is a writer and my son is a chef. My family is very creative and talented. A lot of them use their creativity in hairdressing. Creating hairstyles is an art in itself.

TG: What is the most important thing you have learned during your career as an artist?
SJ: That I have control over how I affect and impact others. My work represents people and how I believe in them. How I believe they have stepped up to a challenge and will continue too.

TG: What are your future goals as an artist?
SJ: To continue creating bodies, sculptures, and painting. I am looking forward to traveling, being inspired, and returning to put my new perspectives and observations into my artwork. I am looking forward to residency with Tama exhibitions, as well as opportunities to work and develop with other artists.

VINNIE BAGWELL

Artist Vinnie Bagwell
(Photo courtesy of Vinnie Bagwell)

New York native, Vinnie Bagwell, is a gifted and untutored artist. Some of Bagwell's commissions include Hartford educator, "Walter 'Doc' Hurley," commissioned by the State of Connecticut, which is the first public artwork of a contemporary African American in the State of Connecticut. A life-sized sculpture of music-icon Marvin Gaye, "'What's Going On!'–Marvin Gaye" was also commissioned by the District of Columbia Department of General Services for the new Marvin Gaye Recreation Center in SE DC.

In 2012, director Ruben Santiago-Hudson sought Vinnie out to create two bas-relief sculptures to enhance a 112-year-old piano for August Wilson's play, "The Piano Lesson" at the Signature Theatre in New York City. At the request of the Alabama Historical Society and the Alabama State Council on the Arts, Vinnie created "Liberté," a 22 h. bronze, to exhibit in the inaugural year-long *Road to Equality: The 1961 Freedom Rides* © exhibition to commemorate the 50th anniversary of the Freedom Rides at the new Freedom Rides Museum in Montgomery in 2011.

Other commissions include, "The Man in the Arena" ©2015, a bronze, life-sized three-quarter bust of President Theodore Roosevelt, commissioned by the DC Government Department of General Services for the Roosevelt Senior High School in Washington, DC, "Legacies" ©2010, commissioned by the City of Memphis for Chickasaw Heritage Park in TN, honors the Chickasaw Native Americans, African Americans, and Hispanic Americans, and "Frederick Douglass Circle" ©2008, commissioned by Hofstra University in Hempstead, NY. A 24" h. maquette of "Frederick Douglass Circle" was Vinnie's 2004 finalist submission for the Frederick Douglass Circle Public-Art Competition for Central Park NW, in New York City. The Highland Beach Historical Society in Maryland purchased it for the centerpiece for the Frederick Douglass Museum and Cultural Center.

Tammy Gibson: It is an honor to speak with you, Ms. Bagwell. Can you please tell me your background and what inspired you to be an artist?
Vinnie Bagwell: I was a child who could draw very well, early on. I grew up during the Civil Rights and Black Power Movements. In my youth, I was very much aware of current events because it was on television and from hearing my parents talk during that era. I met Martin Luther King, Jr., when he came to my church, when I was seven years old. I read The Malcolm X Autobiography when I was ten years old. My mother would take me to my "uncle's" bookstore, and I would select books to read about black history. So, I was aware of black history.

I also had mentors since eight grade: My high-school mentor was the English Chair, Toni Abramson. She challenged me to learn how to write well and take every English class offered at Woodlands High School because "it will open doors because many grown-ups don't write well." I entered college thinking I was going to go to grad school to become a clinician. In my senior year, I was exhausted and decided this was not what I wanted to do. My college mentor, Psychology Chair Dr. George Carter, said, "I don't understand why you are not in the Art Department!"

When I returned to New York after college, I started off working as a social worker. One of my cousins, a photographer, introduced me to a graphic designer, and Harold Esannason became my mentor and groomed me to be self-employed for five years. I used my writing skills and learned all kinds of things that they don't teach you in school.

In 1992, I realized I had had a painting block for seven years. I tried sculpting to "prime the well," and discovered a new passion. At the time, I was 36-years old. I started to look for public art everywhere and I realized that art about African Americans was missing.

I said to myself, "This must be what God wants me to do! Forget painting; this is what I am going to do." However, this was before the internet, and it was impossible to figure out how to find calls for artists, so I wrote a proposal to the City of Yonkers to create a sculpture of Ella Fitzgerald because she had grown up in Yonkers. It ended up becoming the first public artwork of a contemporary African American woman to be commissioned by a municipality in the United States!

Ella Fitzgerald statue in Yorkers, NY.

I left New York for Maryland in 1998. I didn't compete for a public art commission until 2003. I didn't win my first public art competition until 2008. Thus, I returned to New York.

In 2009, the Yonkers City-Council Majority Leader, Patricia McDow, made me aware of the history of enslaved Africans in Yonkers. Researching, I found out that these enslaved Africans were among the first to be manumitted, freed by law, in the United

States, 64 years before the Emancipation Proclamation and that there were no monuments to enslaved Africans. The closest to a memorial was the African Burial Ground in Manhattan.

Thus, the initiative for "The Enslaved Africans' Rain Garden," an urban-heritage sculpture garden, began. It has grown into a major element in an exciting revitalization of the Yonkers Downtown-Waterfront District. The City of Yonkers, ArtsWestchester (the largest non-profit arts council in New York State), New York State Office of Parks, Recreation and Historic Preservation, Yonkers Public Schools, historians, scholars, community-based organizations, and community members partnered with me to develop the creation of the Enslaved Africans' Rain Garden.

The public artwork for this destination project interprets the legacy of enslaved Africans who resided at the Philipse Manor Hall (a New York State historic site). My concept entails five life-sized sculptures; I'Satta, an African woman carrying a bucket of water and fish; Bibi, an older woman gardening; Themba, a boatman, and two children, Sola and Olumide sitting together. The principal for BCT Architects, Bryce Turner, FAIA, NCARB, is responsible for realizing my vision via the development of the site plan and illustrations.

To draw the community into the creative process, I hosted in-studio artists talks with local students and previews of the enlargements before they went to casting. I managed social media engagement and curated a traveling exhibition, all of which established a quantifiable impact on the community. Many contributors were responsible for this effort coming to fruition, such as the City of Yonkers via Federal Community-Development Block Grants, the County of Westchester, New York State Council on the Arts, the National Endowments for the Arts, Arts Westchester, Con Edison, Entergy, and Metro Partners. Nearly an acre of land has been designated for the Enslaved Africans' Rain Garden on the shore of the Hudson River adjacent to Apex (a luxury residential complex). The idea of a rain garden has been chosen to demonstrate the aspects of sustainability and environmental responsibility that make up the design. Construction and installation of artwork will be completed this fall. Once completed, it will be one of the first significant urban-heritage sculpture gardens dedicated to enslaved Africans. A monument to honor the enslaved Africans is long overdue.

TG: What artists inspired you?
VB: Photography inspires me. Photographers have the ability to capture "a Kodak moment." I grew up with that ad campaign. I started making images at 15. Years later, when I look at the images I made in the 70s, 80s, and 90s, I captured the history of my family.

Certain qualities of imagery strike me. Images have power and the question is, do you know what a powerful image looks like? I recognize powerful images.

My daughter is a fantastic artist. When she was five years old, she asked me if there is such a thing as black princesses. I told her, "Of course, there are!" She shot back, "Well, how come you don't see them on TV?" I told her, "Everything is not on TV." She peeped Disney at five! So, what did I do? I made black princesses, black fairies, black mermaids… because I realize you do not see them in the sculpting medium. Black people are beautiful, and it is a shame that we have been marginalized the way we are. My goal is to represent the marginalized people.

TG: You are commissioned to replace the controversial statue of J. Marion Sims, known as "The Father of Gynecology," who experimented on enslaved black women. That public artwork was removed from Fifth Avenue, at 103rd Street outside Central Park, and stored at the Green-Wood Cemetery, where he is buried. Can you discuss the sculpture "The Victory Beyond Sims" that will be installed where the Sims statue was located?
VB: The City of New York removed the sculpture in 2018. Most people don't even know about J. Marion Sims' story. Still, too many people are focusing on him, and not the enslaved women who sacrificed their bodies without anesthesia or

painkillers. There were 12 women he experimented on. Just because we don't know all of their names doesn't diminish the value of their contribution.

"Victory…" highlights African American women, their vital roles in the medical arena, and is a story of healing. As I researched ideas that might be celebrated in the Museum of New York across the street from the site, I realized angels are often depicted in public art. But when I Googled black angels, I could not find any.

I thought New York should have a black angel. At finals, I was the community's choice. There is no higher honor than being valued by the community when you are a public artist. Art in public places is for the community.

The City of New York projected "Victory's…" installation to be sometime in 2021. However, the City has suspended all public artwork until further notice due to the pandemic. All of the public artworks that were scheduled to be created for New York City this year were to celebrate women of color in every borough, as well as the Lyon Family who lived in Seneca Village, a black community that existed before it was turned into Central Park. These artworks need to be created to balance the narrative in the public realm.

Our Governor, Andrew Cuomo, understands the importance and value of public art. He made sure I was designated as an "essential business" to enable the completion of my Sojourner Truth for Poughkeepsie's Walkway Over the Hudson and Bibi, the last sculpture for the Rain Garden, at the beginning of the self-quarantine. He has foresight and understood the importance of getting our stories out.

TG: Why is it that African Americans are not being commissioned for public artwork, especially women?
VB: Well, it is not like we don't have the ability or power. There are a plethora of talented black artists. We can excel in any arena, only if the playing field is leveled. White men have been running public art for centuries. They used art in

public places for propaganda to support white supremacy in this country. Things have been changing. Now, they are changing more faster than expected.

Municipalities in the United States were on the path to access their portfolios, and realizing they don't have women or black people in their public art collections. Many confederate cities are removing offensive public artworks. Cities like Los Angeles, San Francisco, and Boise are pressing on with their plans to celebrate black women in 2020. I am hopeful for New York City.

Black artists have the power to be whatever we want to be. The question is, who is running things and will they let us play? Less than 5% of public artworks in the United States are made by women, and less than that are made by black people. This has to change. We have to do more.

Recently, a woman discovered me on social media and she wrote, "Oh my god, I just discovered your artwork. I've never seen myself in a sculpture before. You made me cry!"

My point is, one of the reasons why people love my work is because they haven't seen enough of themselves in this medium.

When people see my artwork, they can see the time, love, care, and that is what makes them love and respect my work. That is what matters to me. I represent.

VIXON SULLIVAN

Artist Vixon Sullivan
(Photo courtesy of Hannah Swede)

Vixon Sullivan, founder of Vixon Sullivan Art (VSA) was created from the will to bring joy to others through small gifts. His mission is to provide masterful works of art and exceptional service. His company aims to impact gifting culture by crafting treasures that inspire joy in life's everyday moments and special occasions. In VSA's world, nothing is taken for granted, and the beauty found in nature is to remind us to stay uplifted.

Tammy Gibson: What is your background and what inspired you to be a sculptor.
Vixon Sullivan: I'm from Monticello, MS. I graduated from the University of Southern Mississippi with a degree in advertising and a minor in art. I am the youngest of four, and I think that's relevant because, as the youngest, you tend to take on a little bit of everyone's characteristics before you. I think that is where I get most of my creative influence; from my parents and siblings. All of them had their own expression of art, and I think I took on a little bit of each one of them.

After graduating, I worked at Hattiesburg American, where I had about 200 clients that I provided strategies in advertising and marketing. I appreciated that job because it established and allowed me to meet people in the Hattiesburg community. After I resigned from Hattiesburg American, I worked part-time at a frame shop, and when I got laid off, I decided to pursue art full-time. I drew portraits of my clients at Hattiesburg American, and when I resigned from there, I realized that I could not draw fast enough to make a living and that was when I got back into ceramics.

I became involved in The South Mississippi Arts Association, where I was the newsletter editor and later became president for two years. Because I was so involved in the community from Hattiesburg American, to a local framer, to being the President of the South Mississippi Arts Association and volunteering a lot of my time, I got a lot of opportunities to do things for the re-development of Hattiesburg Ward 2 (Twin Forks Rising Redevelopment), that is an organization that is designed to improve the quality of life for the residents and businesses in Hattiesburg. I am a full-time ceramic sculptor and potter. I travel and do shows in Louisiana, Georgia, Mississippi, Alabama, festivals, markets, and display my products in stores.

TG: What artist inspired you?
VS: Salvador Dali inspired me because his work told a story through symbolism. He took reality and merged it with his idea of reality. To me, his art asks the question, "What if."

Vernon Dahmer statue in Hattiesburg, MS.

TG: Was the statue of Vernon Dahmer, who was killed in 1966 for recruiting African Americans to vote in Hattiesburg, MS, your first sculpture?
VS: I have done a few busts and one sculpture in bronze bas-relief for the Twin Forks Rising Monument signs that is a landmark. There are four, located in Hattiesburg, MS.

TG: Did you know about the history of Vernon Dahmer prior to making the statue?
VS: I did not know much about Vernon Dahmer until I was commissioned to do the job. My first response was, I have a lot of learning to do. For me to capture the essence of Vernon Dahmer, I had to learn about who he was.

TG: How did you feel when you were selected to design the Vernon Dahmer statue?
VS: I was excited, but at the same time, I was still very much focused on the understanding that there is work to be done and a lot to learn. I was nervous because I had a lot to live up to, and I wanted to make sure the statue was done right.

TG: What is the height and how long did it take you to complete the statue?
VS: The Vernon Dahmer statue is a bronze, a little bit taller than seven feet tall. Another artist, Ben Watts, and I worked on the statue, and it took four months to complete.

TG: How did you feel at the statue's dedication and unveiling?
VS: Actually, I had to speak at the dedication. I felt responsible for delivering a message that people would be proud of and allow Dahmer's legacy to live on in a non-superficial way. Not just "If you don't vote, you don't count," but feel the same passion that he had and encourage people to feel good about the work they are doing in the community, and to realize that more work still needs to be done.

TG: While doing my research, the majority of African American statues are designed by white sculptors. How do you feel about the lack of African Americans not getting commission work to do African American statues?
VS: It stems from a place of African Americans not necessarily having the opportunity. So, therefore, their resumes do not stack up well against their white counterparts. For me, Vernon Dahmer was my first large bronze. If I was to go and present, "I want to do a sculpture by myself, and another guy who is not African American comes in and says, "Well, I've done ten statues already." A lot of people who employ sculptors are employed from communities they are familiar with, and often, the employers are the people who hold these positions in government and politics. At times, they are not African Americans.

TG: What projects are you working on now?
VS: I am doing my first job in infrastructure to make an artistic bridge, road, or train track. I am also working on renovating my first physical location for my company. I am excited and proud because there are not that many black potters who own a company and be able to distribute to the masses. To have one of the first ceramic studios in Hattiesburg, MS, a black-owned business and to have a diverse customer base, is a great feeling.

TG: What advice would you give to an aspiring sculptor?
VS: Your work and interest are received based on when you have a positive attitude.

LIST OF MONUMENTAL STATUES & MONUMENTS

"I have created nothing really beautiful, really lasting, but if I can inspire one of these youngsters to develop the talent I know they possess, then my monument will be in their work."
- Augusta Savage

"Art must be the quintessence of meaning. Creative art means that you create yourself."
- Meta Vaux Warrick Fuller

"I have always wanted my art to service my people-to reflect us, to relate to us, to stimulate us, to make us aware of our potential. We have to create an art for liberation and for life."
- Elizabeth Catlett

Harold Washington, Chicago, IL
Sculptor: Ed Dwight, Jr.

Sojourner Truth, Battle Creek, MI
Sculptor: Tina Allen

Richard Pryor, Peoria, IL
Sculptor: Preston Jackson

Billie Holiday, Baltimore, MD
Sculptor: James Earl Reid

Adam Clayton Powell, New York, NY
Sculptor: Branly Cadet

Denmark Vessey, Charleston, SC
Sculptor: Ed Dwight, Jr.

Willie Herenton, Memphis, TN
Sculptor: Eddie Dixon

Frederick Douglass, Hempstead, NY
Sculptor: Vinnie Bagwell

Kathleen Cooper Wright, Fort Lauderdale, FL
Sculptor: George Gadson

Twin Forks Rising Bas-Relief, Hattiesburg, MS
Sculptor: Vixon Sullivan

Whitney Young, Frankfort, KY
Sculptor: Ed Hamilton

Martin Luther & Coretta King, Allentown, PA
Sculptor: Ed Dwight, Jr.

A. Philip Randolph, Boston, MA
Sculptor: Tina Allen

Emancipation, Austin, TX
Sculptor: Ed Dwight, Jr.

Harriet Tubman, Boston, MA
Sculptor: Fern Cunningham

Frankie Muse-Freeman, St. Louis, MO
Sculptor: Brian R. Owens

Harriet E. Wilson, Milford, NH
Sculptor: Fern Cunningham

Invisible Man, New York, NY
Sculptor: Elizabeth Catlett

Dizzy Gillespie, Cheraw, SC
Sculptor: Ed Dwight, Jr.

Alex Haley, Knoxville, TN
Sculptor: Tina Allen

Tim Cole, Lubbock, TX
Sculptor: Eddie Dixon

Martin Luther King, Springfield, IL
Sculptor: Geraldine McCullough

Thaddeus Tate, Charlotte, NC
Sculptor: Ed Dwight, Jr.

Marvin Gaye, Washington, D.C.
Sculptor: Vinnie Bagwell

Mahalia Jackson, New Orleans, LA
Sculptor: Elizabeth Catlett

Miles Davis, Alton, IL
Sculptor: Preston Jackson

Harriet Tubman, New York, NY
Sculptor: Alison Saar

Martin Luther King, Jr., Charlotte, NC
Sculptor: Selma Burke

Fred Hampton, Maywood, IL
Sculptor: Preston Jackson

Rosa Parks, Grand Rapids, MI
Sculptor: Ed Dwight, Jr.

Mervyn Dymally, Los Angeles, CA
Sculptor: Nijel Binns

Doris Miller, Waco, TX
Sculptor: Eddie Dixon

Octavius V. Catto, Philadelphia, PA
Sculptor: Branly Cadet

Humiliation, Tulsa, OK
Sculptor: Ed Dwight, Jr.

Louis Armstrong, New Orleans, LA
Sculptor: Elizabeth Catlett

Eternal Presence, Boston, MA
Sculptor: John Wilson

ALABAMA

AUBURN

Bo Jackson
Auburn University
Jordan-Hare Stadium
251 S. Donahue Drive
East Elevator Lobby
Professional NFL and MLB Player.

Cam Newton
Auburn University
251 S. Donahue Drive
Gate 6-7
Professional NFL Player.

Charles Barkley
Auburn Area
250 Beard-Eaves Court
Scholarship Entry
Professional NBA Player.

BIRMINGHAM

4 Little Girls – Four Spirits
Kelly Ingram Park
5th Avenue N. & 16th Street
The bombing of four little girls at the 16th Street Baptist Church.

Children's Crusade
Kelly Ingram Park
5th Avenue N. & 16th Street
1,000 students ditched school and marched downtown, gathering at the 16th Street Baptist Church. More than 600 children were jailed that day.

Eddie Kendricks
4th Avenue & 18th Street N.
Member of the Temptations.

Fred Shuttlesworth
Birmingham Civil
Rights Institute
520 16th Street N.
Minister & civil rights activist.

Ground Zero
Kelly Ingram Park
5th Avenue N. & 16th Street
Police dogs were used to attack marchers.

Martin Luther King, Jr.
Kelly Ingram Park
5th Avenue N. & 16th Street
Minister & civil rights leader.

The Foot Soldier

Kelly Ingram Park
5th Avenue N. & 16th Street
Police dog attacking a young black protester during the Civil Rights Movement.

Three Ministers Kneeling

Kelly Ingram Park
5th Avenue N. & 16th Street
Three ministers kneeling to praying for peace.

Water Cannon

Kelly Ingram Park
5th Avenue N. & 16th Street
Firehosing of school children during the Civil Rights Movement.

DANVILLE

Jesse Owens

Jesse Owens Museum
7109 County Road 203
Owens' nickname was the Buckeye Bullet.

FLORENCE

W.C. Handy

Woodrow Wilson Park
223 E. Tuscaloosa
Blues composer and musician.

HUNTSVILLE

Black Simon Help Jesus

Oakwood University
700 Adventist Boulevard
Center of the University on College Drive
Simon of Cyrene as the man who helped haul Jesus' cross to Calvary Hill.

Buffalo Soldiers Memorial 10th Cavalry

2800 Poplar Avenue
10th Cavalry Sgt. George Berry riding his horse up Cuba's San Juan Hill with the regimental flag.

William Hooper Council

Alabama A&M University
4900 Meridian Street N.
Meridian Street & Drake Drive
Former slave and the first president of Huntsville Normal School, that is now Alabama Agricultural and Mechanical University.

LAFAYETTE

Joe Louis

Chambers County Courthouse
2 Lafayette Street
World heavyweight boxing champion from June 22, 1937 to March 1, 1949.

MARION

Coretta Scott King
Mt. Tabor Church
8747 Coretta Scott
King Highway
*Civil rights activist and the
wife of 1960s civil rights leader
Martin Luther King Jr.*

MOBILE

Cudjoe "Kazoola" Lewis
Union Missionary
Baptist Church
506 Bay Bridge Road
*Survivor of the last slave
ship, Clotilda.*

Unity
Unity Point Park
900 Spring Hill Avenue
*Civil rights activist John
LeFlore and former Mobile
Mayor Joseph Langan and
shaking hands for unity
between blacks and whites.*

MONTGOMERY

Education
201 Monroe Street
*A teacher holding hands with a
boy and girl.*

Guided by Justice
The National Memorial for

Peace and Justice
417 Caroline Street
*Dedication to the women who
sustained the Montgomery
Bus Boycott.*

Nkyinkyim
The National Memorial for
Peace and Justice
417 Caroline Street
*Memory of the Transatlantic
slave trade.*

Rosa Park
Alabama State University
Main Entrance
N. University Street & S.
Jackson Street
*Mother of the Civil Rights
Movement who refused to give
up her seat that sparked the
Montgomery Bus Boycott.*

Rosa Parks
Courts Square on
Dexter Avenue
*Parks investigated Recy
Taylor's 1944 rape case for the
NAACP. Taylor was abducted
and raped by six white men in
Abbeville, AL.*

Rosa Parks*
Rosa Parks Museum
and Library
251 Montgomery Street
Inside the Museum
*Parks was born on February 4,
1913, in Tuskegee, AL.*

SELMA

Civil Rights Leaders
Civil Rights Memorial Park
Broad Street & US
Highway 80
*Monuments of Joseph and
Evelyn Lowery, Hosea
Williams, John Lewis, Amelia
Boynton Robinson and
Marie Foster.*

Martin Luther King, Jr.
Brown Chapel
A.M.E. Church
410 Martin Luther
King Street
*King entered college at the
age of 15.*

TUSKEGEE

George Washington Carver
Tuskegee University
Carver Museum
1200 W. Montgomery Road
*Scientist, botanist, inventor,
and environmentalist who
revolutionized Southern
agriculture.*

ARIZONA

FORT HUACHUCA

Buffalo Solider
Buffalo Soldier Legacy Plaza
Smith Avenue &
Winrow Street
*Black troops that served at
Fort Huachuca.*

MESA

Duke Ellington
Trailhead Members Club
7900 E. Eagle Crest Drive
*Awarded the Presidential
Medal of Freedom in 1969.*

George Washington Carver
Las Sendas
Southwestern Corner &
Sonoran Heights Parke
*Carver was born in
Diamond, MO.*

Harriet Tubman
Las Sendas
Corner of East Saddleback &
Eagle Crest Drive
*Conductor of the Underground
Railroad and an armed scout
and spy for the United States
Army during the American
Civil War.*

Paul Robeson
Las Sendas
East Corner of Harriet
Tubman Children's Parke
Athlete, singer, actor, and
advocate for civil rights.

PARADISE VALLEY

4 Little Girls
4027 East Lincoln Drive
The bombing of four little
girls at the 16th Street
Baptist Church.

George Washington Carver
George Washington
Carver Museum and
Cultural Center
415 E Grant Street
Carver was the first African
American student at Iowa State.

ARKANSAS

FORT SMITH

Bass Reeves
Ross Pendergraft Park
200 Garrison Avenue
Black Deputy U.S. Marshals
west of the Mississippi River.

HELENA

U.S. Colored Troops
Freedom Park
750 South Biscoe
Soldiers of the Union Army
and participated in the Battle
of Helena on July 4, 1863.

LITTLE ROCK

Harriet Tubman
Ferry Street & President
Clinton Avenue Harriet
Tubman was born
Araminta Ross.

Little Rock Nine
Testament
Arkansas State Capitol
4th Street & Martin Luther
King Drive
Nine students involved in the
desegregation of Little Rock
Central High School in 1957.

CALIFORNIA

ANAHEIM

Tiger Woods
Tiger Woods
Learning Center
1 Tiger Woods Way
Professional golfer.

BRENTWOOD

Wendell Brown
12011 San Vicente Boulevard
Homeless poet.

Martin Luther King, Jr.
Court House Park
1100 Van Ness Avenue
King was the youngest man to receive the Nobel Peace Prize.

CHICO

Martin Luther King, Jr.
Community Park
1900 Dr. Martin Luther King Jr. Parkway
King received his doctorate in systematic theology.

HOLLYWOOD

Dorothy Dandridge
Hollywood Boulevard &
LaBrea Avenue
First African American woman to be nominated for an Academy Award for best actress.

DAVIS

Martin Luther King, Jr.*
University of
California–Davis
King Hall
400 Mrak Hall Drive
King was imprisoned nearly 30 times.

LAGUNA HILLS

Florence Griffith Joyner
Saddleback Memorial
Medical Center
24411 Health Center Drive
Track and field athlete.

LA JOLLA

Sojourner Truth
University of California
– San Diego
Thurgood Marshall Campus
Economics Hall &
Sequoyah Hall
Abolitionist and women's rights activist.

FRESNO

Martin Luther King, Jr.
Fresno State University
Peace Garden
2351 E. Barstow Avenue
King's national home is a national historical site.

Thurgood Marshall
Thurgood Marshall College
Administration
9500 Gilman Drive
Associate Justice of the
Supreme Court of the
United States.

LONG BEACH

Martin Luther King, Jr.
Martin Luther King, Jr. Park
1950 Lemon Avenue
Rhea Street &
Lemon Avenue
King was ordained as a Baptist
minister in 1948.

LOS ANGELES

Celes King III
Martin Luther King Jr. &
Crenshaw Boulevards
Bail bondsman &
community advocate.

Earvin "Magic" Johnson
Staples Center
1111 S. Figueroa Street
NBA Hall of Famer.

Elgin Baylor
Staples Center
1111 S. Figueroa Street
NBA Hall of Famer.

Hank Gathers
Loyola Marymount
University
Gersten Pavilion
1 Loyola Marymount
University
College basketball player at
Loyola Marymount University.

Jackie Robinson
Las Angeles
Dodger Stadium
1000 Vin Scully Avenue
First African American to play
in the Major Leagues.

Jackie Robinson 42
University of California,
Los Angeles
John R. Wooden Recreation
and Sports Center
221 Westwood Plaza
Robinson was born on January
31, 1919, in Cairo, GA.

Jackie Robinson
Jackie Robinson Stadium
100 Constitution Avenue
Robinson was drafted in the
Army in 1942.

Kareem Abdul Jabbar
Staples Center
1111 S. Figueroa Street
NBA Hall of Famer.

Mervyn M. Dymally
Charles R. Drew University
Mervyn M. Dymally School
of Nursing

1748 E. 118th Street
Congressman or California's
31st District in the U.S. House
of Representatives from 1981
until 1993.

Mother of Humanity
Watts Labor Community
Action Committee
10950 S. Central Avenue
Tribute to peace, a mother's
loving-kindness, and
the singularity of the
human family.

Shaquille O'Neal
Staples Center
1111 S. Figueroa Street
NBA Hall of Famer.

MISSION VIEJO

Florence Griffith Joyner
Florence Joyner
Olympiad Park
22760 Olympiad Road
Track and field athlete.

OAKLAND

Cottrell Laurence Dellums
Jack London Square Station
245 2nd Street
Pullman Porter and Union
Organizer for the Brotherhood
of Sleeping Car Porters.

Donald P. McCullum
Ronald V. Dellums
Federal Building
1301 Clay Street
Judge and the first African
American city attorney of
Berkeley, CA.

Frederick Douglass*
African American Museum
and Library at Oakland
659 14th Street
Human rights leader in the
anti-slavery movement and
the first African American
citizen to hold a high U.S.
government rank.

Remember Them:
Champions for Humanity
Henry J. Kaiser
Memorial Park
1900 Rashida
Muhammad Street
Extraordinary people from
every corner of the globe.

PASADENA

Jackie & Mack Robinson
100 N. Garfield Avenue
Located on Garfield Avenue,
north of Union Street, across
from City Hall
Mack Robinson was the older
brother to Jackie Robinson.
Mack Robinson, finished
second to Olympic legend Jesse

Owens in the 200 meters in the 1936 Berlin Games.

Jackie Robinson
Rose Bowl Stadium
1001 Rose Bowl Drive
Played football at Pasadena Junior College and UCLA.

PITTSBURG

Martin Luther King
Martin Luther King Jr.
Junior High School
2012 Carion Court
Minister & civil rights leader.

POWAY

Tony Gwynn
Lake Poway Park
14644 Lake Poway Road
MLB Hall of Famer.

RIVERSIDE

Martin Luther King, Jr.
Downtown Riverside
3900 Main Street
King was president of The Southern Christian Leadership Conference.

SAN BERNADINO

Martin Luther King, Jr.
City Hall of the City of San Bernardino
300 N. "D" Street
In 1963, King wrote "Letter from Birmingham, Jail."

Rosa Parks*
Rosa Parks State
Memorial Building
464 W. 4th Street
Parks was a member of the Montgomery chapter of the NAACP.

SAN DIEGO

Breaking the Chain
First Avenue &
Harbor Drive
Dedicated to Martin Luther King, Jr.

Malcolm X*
Malcolm X Library
5148 Market Street
Muslim minister and human rights activist.

SAN FRANCISCO

Tony Gwynn
Peto Park
100 Park Boulevard
MLB Hall of Famer.

William A. Leidesdorff, Jr.
Pine Street &
Leidesdorff Street
Founding Fathers of California
and a successful businessman.

Willie Convoy
Giant Stadium – AT&T Park
24 Willie Mays Plaza
MLB Hall of Famer.

Willie Mays
Giant Stadium – AT&T Park
24 Willie Mays Plaza
MLB Hall of Famer.

SAN JOSE

Olympic Black Power
San Jose University
1 Washington Square
Between Clark Hall &
Tower Hall
John Carlos and Tommie
Smith's Black Power salute at
the 1968 Olympics.

SOUTH BERKELEY

William Byron Rumford
Sacramento Street &
Ashby Street
First African American
elected to a state public office
in Northern California and
pharmacist.

COLORADO

COLORADO SPRINGS

Charlie Sampson
PRCA Hall of Fame Garden
101 Pro Rodeo Drive
First African American to
win a World Title in the
Professional Rodeo Cowboys
Association.

Fannie Mae Duncan
190 S. Cascade Avenue
Community activist and
owner of the Cotton Club in
downtown Colorado Springs.

Tuskegee Airmen
U.S. Air Force Academy
Harmon Hall
3116 Academy Drive
First black servicemen to serve
as military aviators in the U.S.
armed forces.

William Seymour
215 S. Tejon Street
First African American to
serve on a jury in the El Paso
County Courthouse and a
founding member of St. John's
Baptist Church; the first black
Baptist Church built in the
Colorado Springs area.

DENVER

Darrent Williams
Darrent Williams
Teen Center
4397 Crown Boulevard
NFL football player.

Dr. Justina L. Ford
2335 Arapahoe Street
The first licensed African American woman doctor in Colorado from 1902-1952 delivering 7,000 babies.

Martin Luther King, Jr.
"Standing on the Shoulders"
2301 E. 17th Avenue
Dr. King is standing on the shoulders of Rosa Parks, Gandhi, Frederick Douglass, and Sojourner Truth.

PUEBLO

Martin Luther King, Jr. & Emmett Till
2713 N. Grand Avenue
Minister & civil rights leader & civil rights martyr.

CONNECTICUT

BRIDGEPORT

Lewis Latimer
Margaret E. Morton
Government Center
999 Broad Street
Inventor and patent draftsman for the lightbulb and the telephone.

HARTFORD

Emancipation
Lincoln Financial
Sculpture Walk
300 Columbus Boulevard
Upper Level
Slaves celebrate their newfound freedom.

Toward Union Line
Lincoln Sculpture Walk
300 Columbus Boulevard
Lower Level
A young woman walking north toward Union lines symbolizing the trials and tribulations of life as a former enslaved person.

Walter "Doc" Hurley
Woodland Street &
Ridgefield Street
War World II Veteran who

helped hundreds of students attend college.

NEW HAVEN

Amistad
165 Church St
Tribute to Joseph Cinque and the other Mende Africans who escaped slavery in 1839 by commandeering the Spanish ship La Amistad.

STAMFORD

Jackie Robinson
Jackie Robinson
Park of Fame
Main Street & High Street
Robinson was the founder of Freedom National Bank in Harlem in 1964.

DELAWARE

DOVER

Dr. Jerome Holland
Delaware State University
University Pedestrian Mall
1200 N. Dupont Highway
6th President of Delaware State University and the first African American to sit on the

board of the New York Stock Exchange in 1972.

SALISBURY

Harriet Tubman
Salisbury University
Teacher Education and
Technology Center
1101 Camden Avenue
Harriet Tubman's nickname was Moses.

WILMINGTON

African American Medal of Honor
Brandywine Park
18th Street &
Baynard Boulevard
Dedicated to the 87 soldiers who were awarded the U.S. Medal of Honor.

Clifford Brown
Kirkwood Park
701 W. 11th Street
Bebop jazz trumpeter.

Father and Son
Spencer Plaza
800 N. French Street
A young man holding a sleeping child.

Harriet Tubman
Tubman-Garrett

Riverfront Park
40 Rosa Parks Drive
Harriet Tubman died on
March 10, 1913.

Louis L. Redding
Louis L. Redding City
County Building
800 N. French Street
Delaware's first African
American attorney.

Judy Johnson
Frawley Stadium
801 Shipyard Drive
Negro League Player.

DISTRICT
OF COLUMBIA

WASHINGTON

African American Civil
War Monument
1925 Vermont Avenue, NW
200,000 soldiers of the
U.S. Colored Troops who
served during the Civil War
(1861-1865).

A. Philip Randolph*
Washington Union Station
Between Amtrak & MARC
departure level
Was once called "The Most
Dangerous Negro in America."

Benjamin Banneker*
National Museum of African
American History & Culture
1400 Constitution
Avenue N.W.
Mathematician, astronomer,
inventor, and compiler
of almanacs.

Carter G. Woodson
Carter G. Woodson
Memorial Park
Intersection of Rhode
Island Avenue
9th Street & Q Street, NW
Father of Black History Month.

Clara Brown*
National Museum of African
American History & Culture
1400 Constitution
Avenue N.W.
Entrepreneur, philanthropist
and humanitarian in
Denver, CO.

Duke Ellington
Howard Theatre
Florida Avenue &
T Street NW
Ellington was born on April 29,
1899, in Washington, D.C.

Elizabeth Freeman*
National Museum of African
American History & Culture
1400 Constitution
Avenue N.W.
Born "Mum Bett"was the

first enslaved woman to file a lawsuit for freedom in the state of Massachusetts.

Emancipation Memorial
Lincoln Park
East Capitol Street between 11th & 13th Street NE
Lincoln shows him with the Emancipation Proclamation in his right hand and holding his left hand over the head of a liberated slave kneeling at his feet.

Frederick Douglass*
U.S. Capitol Visitor Center Emancipation Hall
Human rights leader in the anti-slavery movement and the first African American citizen to hold a high U.S. government rank.

Jackie Robinson*
National Museum of African American History & Culture
1400
Constitution Avenue NW
Robinson fundraised for the freedom riders during the Civil Rights Movement.

Jesse Owens*
National Museum of African American History & Culture
1400
Constitution Avenue NW
American track-and-field

athlete, Jesse Owens, won four gold medals at the 1936 Berlin Olympic Games.

John Thompson*
John Thompson
Jr. Intercollegiate
Athletic Center
3700 O Street, NW
College basketball coach for the Georgetown Hoyas.

Josh Gibson
Nationals Park
1500 S. Capitol Street SE
South Capital Street & Potomac Avenue
Negro league baseball catcher.

Marion Barry
1350 Pennsylvania Avenue, N.W.
13½ Street & Pennsylvania Avenue
Mayor of D.C.

Martin Luther King, Jr.
1964 Independence Avenue, SW
In 1963, King was named Time magazine's Man of the Year.

Martin Luther King, Jr.*
U.S. Capitol Visitor Center
Rotunda Hall
King was assassinated April 4, 1968.

Marvin Gaye
Bank Place NE &

62nd Street NE
Motown singer.

Mary McCleod Bethune
Lincoln Park
East Capitol Street between
11th & 13th Street NE
Educator and activist, serving as president of the National Association of Colored Women and founding the National Council of Negro Women.

Michael Jordan*
National Museum of African American History & Culture
1400 Constitution Avenue NW *NBA Hall of Famer.*

Nannie Burrough
The Monroe School
601 50th Street, NE
Educator, religious leader, social activist, and the founder of National Trade and Professional Training School for Women and Girls.

Phillis Wheatley*
National Museum of African American History & Culture
1400
Constitution Avenue NW
First published African American female poet.

Robert Smalls*
National Museum of African American History & Culture
1400

Constitution Avenue NW
Born into slavery who became a U.S. Congressman in South Carolina.

Rosa Parks*
U.S. Capitol Visitor Center
Sanctuary Hall
Parks died on October 24, 2005. She was the first woman to lie in state at the U.S. Capitol.

Sojourner Truth*
Capitol Visitor Center
Emancipation Hall
Former slave and an advocate for equality and justice.

Spirit of Freedom
10th Street & U Street
Three infantrymen and a sailor defending Freedom on one side and a soldier with his family on the other.

Students Aspire
Howard University
2400 6th Street, NW
Lewis K. Downing Building
Two students holding up a medallion with arms outstretched supporting one another.

Three Soldiers Monument
5 Henry Bacon Drive, NW
Three soldiers represent the diversity of the US military by including a Caucasian,

*African American, and
Latino American.*

Venus and Serena Williams*
National Museum of African
American History & Culture
1400 Constitution
Avenue, NW
Professional tennis players.

FLORIDA

BOCA RATON

Martin Luther King, Jr.
200 Ruby Street
*President Reagan signed a law,
making Martin Luther King,
Jr.'s birthday a federal holiday.*

COCOA

Melvin Morris
Riverfront Park
*In 1969, Morris led an advance
across enemy lines near Chi
Lang, Vietnam to retrieve a
fallen comrade and destroyed
an enemy force that pinned
his battalion from a series
of bunkers.*

CORAL SPRINGS

Martin Luther King, Jr.
Northwest Regional Library
3151 N. University Drive
*King was a member of Alpha
Phi Alpha Fraternity, Inc.*

DAYTONA BEACH

Jackie Robinson
105 E. Orange Avenue
*Robinson died on
October 24, 1972.*

Mary McCleod Bethune
Bethune-Cookman
University
640 Dr. Mary McCleod
Bethune Boulevard
*Organized President Franklin
Roosevelt's Federal Council
on Negro Affairs, unofficially
known as the "Black Cabinet."*

FORT LAUDERDALE

Kathleen Cooper Wright
2000 W.
Commercial Boulevard
*First African American
School Board member of
Boward County.*

Sankofa
Sistrunk Park
200 N.W. 6th Street

Looking back and celebrating the past while looking forward to planning the future.

The Bridge
African American Research
Library & Cultural Center
2650 Sistrunk Boulevard
The struggles of African Americans on their quest to freedom.

FORT MYERS

2nd Regiment Infantry US Colored Troops
Centennial Park
2100 Edwards Drive
Black Union troops defended Fort Myers from Confederate attack.

GREENVILLE

Ray Charles
Haffye Hays Park
140 Broad Street
Pioneer of soul music, integrating R&B, gospel, pop and country.

HOLLYWOOD

Martin Luther King, Jr.
Martin Luther King
Jr. Community

Center Gymnasium
2400 Charleston Street
King witness President Johnson sign the Civil Rights Act of 1964 into law.

JACKSONVILLE

Buck O'Neil
J.P. Small Park
1701 Myrtle Avenue N
First baseman and manager in the Negro American League.

Bullet Bob Hayes
A. Philip Randolph
Heritage Park
1096 A. Philip
Randolph Boulevard
Olympic sprinter turned American football wide receiver in the National Football League for the Dallas Cowboys.

Martin Luther King, Jr.
University of North Florida
1 University of North
Florida Drive
Peace Plaza
Martin Luther King, Jr. and Coretta Scott were married on June 18, 1953.

KEY WEST

The Forgotten Soldier
Eisenhower Drive &

Truman Avenue
*Soldiers who served
from Key West.*

MIAMI

Toussaint Louverture
Northeast 2nd Avenue &
62nd Street
Leader of the Haitian
Revolution.

ORLANDO

Bob Marley
Universal City Walk –
Upper Level
6000 Universal Boulevard
*Jamaican reggae singer,
songwriter, musician, and
guitarist.*

Tuskegee Airmen
Orlando Science Center
777 E. Princeton Street
*First black servicemen to serve
as military aviators in the U.S.
armed forces.*

PENSACOLA

Martin Luther King, Jr.
50 N. Palafox Street
Palafox Street &
Garden Street

*King attended Morehouse
College in 1944.*

POMPANO BEACH

Family Roots
520 NW 3rd Street
*Tribute to "preservation of
family heritage and identity"–
going back to the past to
appreciate the present and look
forward to the future.*

ST. AUGUSTINE

St. Augustine Foot Soldiers
Plaza De La Constitucion
King Street &
Charlotte Street
*Honors people who marched
to advance the cause of civil
rights in St. Augustine in
1963 and 1964.*

ST. LEO

A Spirit of Belonging
St. Leo University
33701 State Road 52
*Benedictine monks who
founded the institution
admitted a black student,
Rudolph Antorcha, even
though integration was not yet
legal in Florida.*

TALLAHASSEE

Charles K. Steele
Tennessee Street &
Adams Street
Civil rights leader and
organizer of the 1956
Tallahassee bus boycott.

Fred Douglas Lee
Macomb Street &
Georgia Street
1st African American police
officer in Tallahassee.

Integration
Florida State University
600 W. College Avenue
Woodward Plaza
Florida State University
integrated in 1962. Maxwell
Courtney, the first African
American to graduate from
FSU; Fred Flowers, the first
African American to wear
an FSU athletic uniform;
and Doby Flowers, Florida
State's first African American
homecoming princess.

Jake Gaither
Florida A&M University
Jake Gaither Stadium
1601 S. Martin Luther
King Drive
Florida A&M head
football coach.

TAMPA

Benjamin E. Mays
The Tampa Convention
Center – Water Side
333 S. Franklin Street
Mays was born on August 1,
1894, in Epworth, SC.

Blanche Armwood
The Tampa Convention
Center – Water Side
333 S. Franklin Street
First African American woman
from Florida to graduate
from an accredited law school,
Howard University.

Cyril Blythe Andrews
The Tampa Convention
Center – Water Side
333 S. Franklin
First African American to be
appointed to the Hillsborough
County Civil Service Board,
resurrected the Florida
Sentinel Bulletin.

Edward Daniel Davis
The Tampa Convention
Center – Water Side
333 S. Franklin Street
Author, businessman,
and educator. He helped
desegregate the University of
Florida, raise the salary pay of
black teachers on the same level
as white, and helped increase
voter registration.

Garfield Devoe (G.D.) Rogers
The Tampa Convention Center – Water Side
333 S. Franklin Street
Business owner of Tampa's Central Industrial (Life) Company, an agency that sold policies to blacks, Rogers Hotel, Rogers Dining Room, invested in a beach resort and register African Americans to vote.

Lee Roy Selmon
Florida Avenue & Brorein Street
NFL Hall of Famer.

Martin Luther King, Jr.
University of South Florida
Martin Luther King Plaza
4202 E. Fowler Avenue
King received his first honorary degree from Morehouse president, Benjamin E. Mays.

Moses White
The Tampa Convention Center – Water Side
333 S. Franklin Street
Known as the "Mayor of Central Avenue" because of his prowess as a businessman, community leader, and philanthropist.

Paulina Pedroso
The Tampa Convention Center – Water Side
333S. Franklin Street
Prominent female leader of Cuba's 1895 revolution against Spain.

WEST PALM BEACH

Martin Luther King, Jr.
Currie Park
2200 N. Flagler Drive
In 1959, King delivers the commencement address at Morehouse College.

WINTER PARK

Richard R. Hall, Jr.
Hannibal Square Heritage Center
Hannibal Square & New England Avenue
Tuskegee Airmen.

GEORGIA

ALBANY

Ray Charles
146 S. Front Street
Born on September 23, 1930.

ATLANTA

Andrew Young
Andrew Young International Boulevard & Spring Street
Civil rights activist & Mayor of Atlanta.

Behold
450 Auburn Avenue, NE
African tradition of a father holding up his newborn to the sky that symbolizes King's bravery, courage and dignity.

Benjamin Mays
Morehouse College
Sale Hall
830 Westview Drive, SW
Mays was a mentor to Dr. Martin Luther King, Jr.

Booker T. Washington
Washington High School
45 Whitehouse Drive, SW
Washington Place & White House Drive
Washington wrote his autobiography "Up from Slavery."

Charles Drew
Drew Charter School
300 E. Lake Boulevard, SE
Physician and surgeon.

Charles Lincoln Harper
Ashby Garden Park
Ashby Circle & Mayson

Turner Road
First Principal of Booker T. Washington School.

Dominique Wilkins
Philips Arena
1 Philips Drive
NBA Hall of Famer.

Hank Aaron
SunTrust Park
Monument Grove
755 Battery Avenue, SE
MLB Hall of Famer.

Hank Aaron
Turner Field
755 Hank Aaron Drive, SE
MLB Hall of Famer.

Homage to King
Ponce de Leon Avenue NE & Freedom Parkway
Minister and civil rights leader.

John Wesley Dobbs
John Wesley Dobbs Plaza
Auburn Avenue & Fort Street
Unofficial "Mayor" of Auburn Avenue.

Man & Daughter
Entrance of Underground Atlanta
An African American man stands carrying a young African American girl in his arms.

Martin Luther King, Jr.
Georgia State Capitol
206 Washington Street, SW
Piedmont Avenue & Martin
Luther King Jr Drive
The time is always right to do
what is right – 1965 Oberlin
College commencement speech.

Martin Luther King, Jr.
Morehouse Chapel
830 Westview Drive, SW
In 1966, King delivers keynote
address in celebration of
Morehouse's 100th anniversary.

Ronald Yancey
Georgia Institute of
Technology
G. Wayne Clough
Undergraduate
Learning Commons
The first black student to
graduate from Georgia Tech.

Rosa Parks
Georgia Institute of
Technology
Harrison Square
Tech Tower & Cherry Street
Parks became a deaconess at the
African Methodist Episcopal
Church in Detroit, MI.

The Three Pioneers
Georgia Institute of
Technology
Harrison Square
Tech Tower & Cherry Street

First three students
who enrolled at Tech in
September 1961.

Unity
Morris Brown College
643 Martin Luther
King Drive, SW
Honoring the legacy of the
HBCUs and its embrace of the
Westside community.

W.E.B. DuBois
Clark Atlanta
223 James P.
Brawley Drive, SW
Sociologist, historian,
civil rights activist, and
Pan-Africanist.

AUGUSTA

James Brown
James Brown Boulevard &
8th Street
Godfather of Soul.

Lucy Craft Laney
1116 Phillips Street
A school teacher and educator
who opened a school for
African American students in
the South in the late 1800s.

KENNESAW

Martin Luther King, Jr.
Kennesaw State University
Social Science Building &
Student Center
1000 Chastain Road
Dr. Benjamin E. Mays
delivered King's eulogy.

MACON

Otis Redding
Ocmulgee Heritage Trail
Riverside Drive &
MLK Boulevard
Soul singer of the 1960s.

MILTON

Milty's Realm
Milton Library
430 E. High Street
Pony being fed an apple by a
young boy while a happy little
girl sits on his back.

WARNER ROBINS

Eugene Bullard
Museum of Aviation
1942 Heritage Boulevard
First African American who
fought for the French Foreign
Legion during World War II,

Tuskegee Airmen and paved the
way for the desegregation of the
United States military.

WASHINGTON

Austin Dabney
The Square
Spring Street & Robert
Toombs Avenue
Georgia slave, earned freedom
in exchange for his service in
the patriot army.

ILLINOIS

ALTON

Miles Davis
Piasa Street & Belle Street
Jazz musician.

AURORA

Marie Wilkinson
Santori Library
101 S. River Street
Benton Street & Lake Street
Children & civil rights activist.

CHICAGO

Dr. Georgiana
Rose Simpson

University of Chicago
Mandel Hall
1131 E. 57th Street
First black women in the U.S.
to receive a doctorate.

Ernie Banks
Wrigley Field
1060 W. Addison Street
MLB Hall of Famer.

Frank Thomas*
U.S. Cellular Field
Outfield Concourse
333 W. 35th Street
MLB Hall of Famer.

Great Northern Migration
26th Street & King Drive
African Americans who
migrated to Chicago in the
early 20th century in search of
greater freedom.

Gwendolyn Brooks
Gwendolyn Brooks Park
4542 S. Greenwood Avenue
Poet, author, teacher, and the
first African American to win
a Pulitzer Prize.

Harold Baines*
U.S. Cellular Field
Outfield Concourse
333 W. 35th Street
MLB Hall of Famer.

Harold Washington
47th Street & King Drive
Chicago's first Black Mayor.

John Baptiste DuSable
Pioneer Court &
Chicago River
Founder of Chicago.

Martin Luther King, Jr.
Martin Luther King, Jr.
Roller Rink
1219 W. 76th Street
King's body was carried from
Ebenezer Baptist Church to
Morehouse campus for the
final funeral.

Martin Luther King, Jr.
6743 S. Kedzie Avenue
"Out of the mountain of despair,
a stone of hope." – I Have A
Dream speech.

Michael Jordan
United Center
1901 W. Madison Street
Near Gate 5
NBA Hall of Famer.

Minnie Minoso*
U.S. Cellular Field
Outfield Concourse
333 W. 35th Street
Inside Stadium
First black player of the
Chicago White Sox.

Paul Laurence Dunbar
Dunbar Park
200 E. 31st Street
Poet and playwriter.

Scottie Pippen*
United Center
1901 W. Madison Street
Gate 7
NBA Hall of Famer.

Victory Monument
35th & Martin Luther
King, Jr. Drive
Honoring the achievements
of the Eighth Regiment of the
Illinois National Guard, an
African American unit that
served in France during World
War I as part of the 370th
U.S. Infantry.

Walter Dyett
Walter Dyett High School
3000 S. Martin Luther
King, Jr. Drive
49th Street & State Street
A music educator for the
Chicago Public Schools.

Walter Payton
Soldier Field Stadium
1410 Museum
Campus Drive
Gate 0
NFL Hall of Famer.

DECATUR

African American Civil War
Williams Street &
Water Street

Soldiers who fought and died in
defense of emancipation.

JOLIET

Katherine Dunham
Jefferson Street &
Scott Street
Dancer, songwriter, and
choreographer.

Underground
Railroad Hero
Chicago Street &
McDonough Street
The Underground Railroad
ran through Joliet to harbor
fugitive slaves.

MAYWOOD

Fred Hampton
Fred Hampton Family
Aquatic Center
300 Oak Street
Chairman of the Illinois
Chapter of the Black
Panther Party.

NORMAL

Doug Collins-Will
Robinson Statue
Illinois State University
Redbird Arena
100 N. University Street

Head basketball coach Will Robinson, the first African American head basketball coach in NCAA Division I history and player Doug Collins.

OAK PARK

Percy L. Julian
Scoville Park
800 Lake Street
Chemist who synthesize who pioneered the industrial scale chemical synthesis of medicinal drugs as cortisone, steroids, and birth control pills.

PEORIA

Knockin' on Freedom's Door
Liberty Street &
Jefferson Avenue
Pettengill House was a safe house for fugitive slaves along the Underground Railroad to freedom.

Richard Pryor
Washington Street &
State Street
Groundbreaking comedian.

SPRINGFIELD

Martin Luther King, Jr.
Second Avenue &
Capitol Avenue
The Martin Luther King, Jr. Chapel was dedicated by Ambassador Andrew Young in 1978.

INDIANA

ANDERSON

Johnny Anderson
Anderson High School
4610 Madison Avenue
Harlem Globetrotter.

Martin Luther King, Jr.
Martin Luther King Park
West 22nd &
Madison Avenue
The King statue was unveiled in 1984 on the King Chapel Plaza at Morehouse College.

BLOOMINGTON

Celebrating Perfection
Simon Skjodt Assembly Hall
1001 E. 17th Street
1975-76 IU team, Bobby Wilkerson, Kent Benson, Scott May, Quinn Buckner, Jim Crews, and Tom Abernethy

finished the regular season with a perfect 32-0.

George Taliaferro
Indiana University
George Taliaferro Plaza
107 S. Indiana Avenue
First African American drafted by a National Football League.

Tournament Dominance
Simon Skjodt Assembly Hall
1001 E. 17th Street
Former IU player Isiah Thomas's layup in the 1981 NCAA Men's Basketball National Championship game against North Carolina.

Two Pioneers Breaking the Unwritten Rule
Simon Skjodt Assembly Hall
1001 E. 17th Street
IU Coach Branch
McCracken and former IU player Bill Garrett. Garrett was the first African American to play men's basketball in the Big Ten Conference.

GARY

Richard Hatcher
Gary City Hall
401 Broadway
First black mayor of the City of Gary, IN.

Tuskegee Airmen
6918 Oak Avenue
First black servicemen to serve as military aviators in the U.S. armed forces.

INDIANAPOLIS

DeMarus Beasley
Children's Museum
Indianapolis
Riley Children's Health
Sports Legends Experience
3000 N. Meridian Street
Professional soccer player.

Hank Aaron
Children's Museum
Indianapolis
Riley Children's Health
Sports Legends Experience
3000 N. Meridian Street
MLB Hall of Famer.

Landmark for Peace
1702 Broadway Street
Robert Kennedy gave his memorable speech the night King was assassinated in 1968.

Mamie Johnson
Children's Museum
Indianapolis
Riley Children's Health
Sports Legends Experience
3000 N. Meridian Street
Female Negro League

player who played for the Indianapolis Clowns.

Marcenia "Toni Stone" Lye
Children's Museum
Indianapolis
Riley Children's Health
Sports Legends Experience
3000 N. Meridian Street
Female Negro League player for the Indianapolis Clowns and was the first woman to play professional baseball as a regular on a big league team.

Oscar Robertson
Children's Museum
Indianapolis
Riley Children's Health
Sports Legends Experience
3000 N. Meridian Street
NBA Hall of Famer.

Reggie Miller
Children's Museum
Indianapolis
Riley Children's Health
Sports Legends Experience
3000 N. Meridian Street
NBA Hall of Famer.

Reggie Wayne
Children's Museum
Indianapolis
Riley Children's Health
Sports Legends Experience
3000 N. Meridian Street
NFL Hall of Famer who played for the Indianapolis Colts.

Tamika Catchings
Children's Museum
Indianapolis
Riley Children's Health
Sports Legends Experience
3000 N. Meridian Street
WNBA Hall of Famer.

Wilma Rudolph
Children's Museum
Indianapolis
Riley Children's Health
Sports Legends Experience
3000 N. Meridian Street
First American woman to win three gold medals at a single Olympics in 1960, at the Summer Games in Rome.

MUNCIE

Hurley Goodall
Firemen's Park
Jackson Street
&Madison Street
Muncie's first African American representative in the Indiana General Assembly, one of the first two African American firefighters in Muncie and the first African American elected to the Muncie Community School Board.

SOUTH BEND

Martin Luther King, Jr. &
Father Theodore Hesburgh
130 S. Main Street
Linden Avenue to Leighton
Plaza downtown
*Father Theodore Hesburgh
and Dr. Martin Luther King
Jr. holding hands, singing, and
fighting for equality.*

UPLAND

Samuel Morris
Taylor University
236 W. Reade Avenue
*Liberian student and
missionary.*

IOWA

AMES

George Washington Carver
Iowa State University
Seed Science Building
Wallace Drive &
Osborn Road
*Carver died January 5, 1943, at
Tuskegee University.*

Jack Trice
Iowa State University
1550 Beardshear Hall
515 Morrill Road

*Born on May 12, 1902 in
Hiram, OH.*

Jack Trice
Iowa State University
Jack Trice Stadium
1732 S. 4th Street
*First African American athlete
from Iowa State College.*

DES MOINES

Clyde Duncan, Sr.
Iowa Hall of Pride
330 Park Street
*Track & Field athlete who won
nine state track titles from
1962 to 1964 while at Des
Moines North High School.*

IOWA FALLS

Joseph P. Gomer
Ellsworth
Community College
1100 College Avenue
Bullock Jones Hall & Reg
Johnson Hall
Tuskegee Airmen.

SIOUX CITY

Evelyn Freeman
Martin Luther King, Jr.
Transportation Center
505 Nebraska Street

First African American teacher in Sioux City.

KANSAS

FORT LEAVENWORTH

6888th Central Postal Directory Battalion
Buffalo Soldier
Memorial Park
290 Stimson Avenue
African American battalion of the Women's Army Corps that sorted mail in a segregated unit during World War II.

Buffalo Soldier
Buffalo Soldier
Memorial Park
290 Stimson Avenue
Commemorate the significant 'firsts' in the history of African American Soldiers and units in the U.S. Army.

Cathay Williams
Richard Allen Cultural
Center & Museum
4th Street & Kiowa Street

412 Kiowa Street
First female Buffalo Soldier.

Colin Powell
Buffalo Soldier
Memorial Park
290 Stimson Avenue

The first African American appointed as the U.S. Secretary of State and Four-Star General in the United States Army.

Henry Ossian Flipper
Buffalo Soldier
Memorial Park
290 Stimson Avenue
First African American to graduate from West Point.
Walter Morris

Buffalo Soldier
Memorial Park
290 Stimson Avenue
The first African American enlisted soldier accepted for airborne duty, original member of the Triple Nickels, the 555th Parachute Infantry Company.

JUNCTION CITY

Buffalo Soldier
Buffalo Soldier Park
18th & Buffalo Soldier Drive
8th and 9th Buffalo Soldier units that were stationed at Fort Riley and the city of Junction City.

WICHITA

The Soda Fountain
Reflection Square Park
Douglas Avenue

between Market Street &
Broadway Street
*1958 Wichita civil rights lunch
counter sit-in.*

KENTUCKY

COVINGTON

James Bradley
Across the Ohio Walkway
*Abolitionist from the northern
Kentucky area and took part
in the Lane Seminary debates
on slavery.*

FRANKFORT

Whitney Young
Kentucky State University
400 E. Main Street
*Civil rights leader, head of the
National Urban League and
graduate of Kentucky State
University.*

LEXINGTON

First Four
University of Kentucky
Commonwealth Stadium
1540 University Drive
*University of Kentucky African
American football players
Nate Northington, Greg Page,
Houston Hogg and Wilbur*

*Hackett integrated football in
the Southeastern Conference.*

LOUISVILLE

Smoke Town
Muhammad Ali Boulevard
& East Chestnut Street
*Giant Boxing Glove
symbolizing the neighborhood
where Muhammad Ali and
other boxers learned the sport
of boxing.*

York, the Slave
Belvedere Riverfront Plaza
129 River Road
*William Clark's slave, who
was an active participant in
the famous Lewis and Clark
Expedition to the Pacific
Northwest.*

RUSSELLVILLE

Alice Allison Dunnigan
East Sixth Street &
Morgan Street
*First African American
female journalist to cover the
White House.*

LOUISIANA

BATON ROUGE

Courteous Uncle Jack
LSU Rural Life Museum
Monroe Garden
4650 Essen Lane
*Recognition of the arduous and
faithful services of the good
darkies of Louisiana.*

Joseph M. Bartholomew
Joseph M. Bartholomew
Golf Course
7514 Congress Drive
*First African American to
design and build a public golf
facility in the United States.*

Joseph S. Clark,
Southern University and
A&M College
Joseph Samuel Clark
Administration Annex
801 Harding Boulevard
*President of Southern
University from
1913 to 1938.*

Shaquille O'Neal
Louisiana State University
Pete Maravich
Assembly Center
NBA Hall of Famer.

GRAMBLING

Charles P. Adams
Grambling State University
Main Street &
Hutchinson Street
*Founding President of
Grambling University.*

Eddie Robinson*
Eddie Robinson Museum
126 Jones Street
*Coached at Grambling State
University for 57 seasons.*

HAMMOND

Walter A. Reed
Cate Square Park
West Robert Street & N.
Oak Street
*First African American
physician within Hammond
and its vicinity.*

LAFAYETTE

Rosa Parks
Rosa Parks
Transportation Center
100 Lee Street
*Parks was voted by Time
Magazine as one of the 100
most influential people of the
20th century.*

NEW ORLEANS

Alexander P. Tureaud, Sr.
A.P. Tureaud Avenue &
Bernard Avenue
Lawyer and civil rights activist.

Allen Toussaint
New Orleans Musical
Legends Park
311 Bourbon Street
*New Orleans musician,
songwriter, arranger and
record producer.*

Congo Square
Louis Armstrong Park
701 N. Rampart Street
*Slaves could perform and
preserve their own cultures
and traditions despite their
masters' desires to "convert" to
their own ways.*

Fats Domino
Music Legend Park
311 Bourbon Street
*Rhythm-and-blues singer who
became one of the first rock-
and-roll stars and who helped
define the New Orleans sound.*

Irma Thomas
New Orleans Musical
Legends Park
311 Bourbon Street
"Soul Queen of New Orleans."

Marching Brass Band
Louis Armstrong Park
701 N. Rampart Street
Salutes the ragtime musician

Martin Luther King Jr.
Martin Luther
King Boulevard &
Claiborne Avenue
*"Darkness cannot drive out
darkness; only light can do that.
Hate cannot drive out hate; only
love can do that."*

**Martin Luther
King Memorial**
Oretha Castle Haley
& Martin Luther
King Boulevard
*Dr. Kings mission to bring
people together of all races.*

Buddy Bolden.
Louis Armstrong
Algiers Ferry Landing
101 Morgan Street
*Jazz trumpeter, composer
and singer.*

Louis Armstrong
Louis Armstrong Park
701 N. Rampart Street
*Armstrong was born
August 4, 1901.*

Mahalia Jackson
Louis Armstrong Park
701 N. Rampart Street
Gospel singer.

Rev. Avery C. Alexander
University Medical Center
New Orleans
2000 Canal Street
*State legislator and civil
rights leader.*

Ruby Bridges
Akili Academy
Courtyard
3811 N. Galvez Street
*First African American child to
desegregate the all-
white William Frantz
Elementary School in 1960.*

Sidney Bechet
Louis Armstrong Park
701 N. Rampart Street
*Jazz saxophonist, clarinetist,
and composer.*

Spirit House
Gentilly Boulevard & St.
Bernard Avenue
*Represents the contributions of
African Americans who were
instrumental in the cultural
and physical development of
New Orleans.*

The Healing Tree
New Orleans East Hospital
5620 Read Boulevard
*Depicts a severed tree
represents (New Orleans) pre-
Katrina while the blue glass
represents water of change. The
new tree that regenerated from*

*the old represents the resilience
to return and rebuild.*

SHREVEPORT

**Huddie "Lead
Belly" Ledbetter**
416 Texas Street
Blues musician.

MAINE

BREWER

Freedom Statue
Chamberlain Freedom Park
State Street & N. Main Street
*Fugitive slaves in the 1800s
made their way to freedom in
Canada by way of Brewer.*

MARYLAND

ANNAPOLIS

Alex Haley
Sidewalk at City
Dock/Harbor
*A writer known as the author of
the 1976 book "Roots."*

Aris T. Allen
Chinquapin Round Road &
Fairfax Road
First African American

Chair of the Maryland Republican Party.

Frederick Douglass*
Maryland State House
Old House of Delegates
100 State Circle
Abolitionist, orator, writer, and statesman.

Harriet Tubman*
Maryland State House
Old House of Delegates
100 State Circle
Harriet Tubman was born on a plantation in Dorchester County, MD.

Martin Luther King, Jr.
Anne Arundel
Community College
101 College Parkway
King was buried at South View cemetery in Atlanta before buried re-interred at the King Center.

Thurgood Marshall
Thurgood Marshall
Memorial Lawyers' Mall /
State House Square,
State Circle
Associate Justice of the Supreme Court of the United States.

BALTIMORE

Billie Holiday
Pennsylvania Avenue &
Lafayette Avenue
Jazz singer.

The Black Soldiers
100 N. Holliday Street
Fayette Street &
Lexington Street
Memory of the Negro war heroes of the United States.

Earl C. "Papa Bear" Banks
Morgan State University
Legends Plaza
1700 E. Cold Spring Lane
College football coach.

Eddie Murray
Baltimore Orioles
Legends Courtyard
333 W. Camden Street
MLB Hall of Famer.

Edward P. Hurt
Morgan State University
Legends Plaza
1700 E. Cold Spring Lane
Head football, basketball, and track coach at Morgan State College from 1929 to 1959.

Frank Robinson
Baltimore Orioles
Legends Courtyard
333 W. Camden Street
MLB Hall of Famer.

Frederick Douglass
Frederick Douglass–Isaac
Myers Maritime Park
1417 Thames Street
South Caroline Street &
Philpot Street
*Book: Narrative of the Life
of Frederick Douglass by
Frederick Douglass.*

Frederick Douglass
Morgan State University
1700 E. Cold Spring Lane
Hillen Road & E. Cold
Spring Lane
*Book: My Bondage and My
Freedom by Frederick Douglass.*

Frederick Douglass
University of Maryland
Hornbake Plaza
620 W. Lexington Street
*Book: Self-Made Men by
Frederick Douglass.*

Ray Lewis
M&T Bank Stadium
1101 Russell Street
NFL Hall of Famer.

Thurgood Marshall
Hopkins Place & West
Pratt Street
*Born July 2, 1908 in
Baltimore, MD.*

EASTON

Frederick Douglass
Talbot County Courthouse

11 N. Washington Street
*Book: What to the Slave
Is the Fourth of July? By
Frederick Douglass.*

LEXINGTON PARK

**United States
Colored Troops**
John C. Lancaster Park
21550 Willows Road
*Commemorates the 700 plus
African American troops in St.
Mary's County, Maryland who
served as soldiers and sailors
in the Union forces during the
American Civil War.*

NATIONAL HARBOR

Frederick Douglass
American Way &
Waterfront Street
*Book: My Escape from Slavery
by Frederick Douglass.*
*Louis Armstrong
American Way & Fleet Street
Armstrong died on July 6, 1971.*

PRINCESS ANNE

William Percy Hytche
University of Maryland
Eastern Shore
Hytche Athletic Center

11868 College
Backbone Road
*President of the University
of Maryland Eastern Shore
for 20 years.*

MASSACHUSETTS

BOSTON

A. Philip Randolph*
Back Bay Station
145 Dartmouth Street
*Civil Rights Leader &
organized the Brotherhood of
Sleeping Car Porters.*

Bill Russell
Boston City Hall Plaza
1 City Hall Square
NBA Hall of Famer.

Crispus Attucks
Boston Common
Between Tremont Street &
Avery Street
*The first casualty of the
American Revolution.*

Emancipation
Park Place & Eliot Street
*Lincoln shows him with the
Emancipation Proclamation
in his right hand and holding
his left hand over the head
of a liberated slave kneeling
at his feet.*

Emancipation
Harriet Tubman Park
Columbus Square &
Pembroke Street
*Honor the 50th anniversary
of the Emancipation
Proclamation.*

Eternal Presence
Harriet Tubman Park
Crawford Street &
Hollander Street
*Commemorates 350 years of
African American presence in
Massachusetts.*

Free At Last
Boston University
Marsh Plaza
One Silber Way
*Mass of birds striving to be
airborne in honor of Martin
Luther King, Jr.*

Harriet Tubman
Harriet Tubman Park
450 Columbus Avenue
Columbus Square &
Pembroke Street
*Around 1844, Harriet Tubman
married John Tubman, a free
black man.*

Phyllis Wheatley
The Boston's
Women Memorial
Commonwealth Avenue &
Fairfield Street

First published African
American female poet.

Rise/Gateway to Boston
Mattapan Square
Blue Hill Avenue &
River Street
*The family on the top
represents Mattapan's current
population which consists
largely of African Americans
and Caribbean Immigrants.*

**The Robert Gould Shaw
and Massachusetts 54th
Regiment Memorial**
Boston Common
Between of Beacon Street &
Park Street
*Memorial to the group of men
who were among the first
African Americans to fight
in that war.*

The Sentinel
Forest Hill Cemetery
95 Forest Hills Avenue
*Tribute to African ancestors
and strong women in her own
family who raised her.*

FLORENCE

Sojourner Truth
Sojourner Truth Memorial
Pine Street & Park Street
*Former slave and an advocate
for equality and justice.*

HYANNIS

Journey
Zion Union Heritage
Museum 276 N. Street
*African American male
holding a globe with his left
hand on Africa and his fingers
pointing to America to reflect
the continuing journeys that
spanned the eras of the slave
trade, abolitionism, and the
civil rights movement. He
has the world of his future in
his hands.*

LINCOLN

Eternal Presence
deCordova Sculpture Park
and Museum
51 Sandy Pond Road
*Commemorates 350 years of
African American presence in
Massachusetts.*

ROXBURY

Father and Son Reading
Roxbury
Community College
1234 Columbus Avenue
Media Arts Center &
Administration Building
*Safe within his father's embrace,
a boy is absorbed within the*

world of a book, held open for him by the man's strong hands.

The Value of Life
Jeep Jones Park
250 Roxbury Street
Honoring the life and deeds of Boston youth who have set an example for their peers by living a good life in the face of adversity.

WORCESTER

Marshall "Major" Taylor
Worcester Public Library
3 Salem Square
World cycling champion in 1899.

MICHIGAN

BATTLE CREEK

Battle Creek Underground Railroad
1 E. Michigan Avenue near W.K. Kellog Residence
Between Capital Avenue & Division Street
Harriet Tubman would carry a gun for protection and a warning for a runaway slave who had second thoughts.

Sojourner Truth
Corner of Division &

Michigan Avenue
In 1851, Sojourner Truth delivered "Ain't I A Woman" speech at a women's convention in Ohio.

DETROIT

Charles A. Hill, Sr.
Hartford Memorial Baptist Church
18700 James
Couzens Freeway
The second pastor of HMBC.

Charles G. Adams*
Hartford Memorial Baptist Church
18700 James
Couzens Freeway
Pastor of HMBC for over 50 years.

Charles H. Wright*
Charles H. Wright Museum of African American History
315 E. Warren Avenue
Detroit physician.

Gateway to Freedom
One Hart Plaza at the Detroit River
45,000 runaway slaves passed through Detroit on their way to freedom in Canada.

Joe Louis*
Cobo Hall, Macomb Room

West Jefferson &
Washington Boulevard
*World heavyweight boxing
champion from June 22, 1937,
to March 1, 1949.*

**Monument to Joe
Louis–The Fist**
5 Woodward Avenue
*Louis was born on May 13,
1914 in Alabama.*

Naomi Long Madgett*
Charles H. Wright Museum
of African American History
315 E. Warren Avenue
*Award-winning poet and
founder of the Detroit based
Lotus Press.*

Willie Horton
Comerica Park
2100 Woodard Avenue
MLB Hall of Famer.

EAST LANSING

Earvin "Magic" Johnson
Michigan State University
Breslin Center
220 Trowbridge Rd
*Attended Michigan State
University from 1977-1979.*

GRAND RAPIDS

Helen Claytor
Grand Rapids
Community College
Dr. Juan R. Olivarez
Student Plaza
143 Bostwick Avenue, NE
*Civil rights activist who
became the first African
American president of the
national YWCA.*

Lyman Parks
Grand Rapids City Hall
300 Monroe Avenue, NW
Mayor of Grand Rapids.

Rosa Parks
Rosa Parks Circle
Monroe Center &
Fulton Street
*Parks attended her first "State
of the Union Address in
January 1999.*

Sojourner Truth
S. Division Street & E.
Michigan Street
*Sojourner Truth was born
Isabella Baumfree in 1797.*

HILLSDALE

Frederick Douglass
Hillsdale College
33 E. College Street
College Street &

Manning Street
*Human rights leader in the
anti-slavery movement and
the first African American
citizen to hold a high U.S.
government rank.*

KALAMAZOO

Circle of Life
Bronson Methodist Hospital
601 John Street
*Two male and two female
dancers each represent a
different ethnicity and point in
the circle of life.*

Martin Luther King, Jr.
507 N. Rose Street
*King was imprisoned
30+ times.*

YPSILANTI

Harriet Tubman
Ypsilanti District Library
229 W. Michigan Avenue
*Harriet Tubman established the
Home for The Aged in 1908.*

MINNESOTA

DULUTH

**Clayton Jackson
McGhie Memorial**
E. 1st Street & N. 2nd Street
*The 1920 Duluth lynchings of
three African American circus
workers, Elias Clayton, Elmer
Jackson, and Isaac McGhie for
a crime they did not commit.*

Joseph P. Gomer
Duluth International Airport
Departure Level
4931 Airport Road
Tuskegee Airmen.

MINNEAPOLIS

Kirby Puckett
Target Field
1 Twins Way
MLB Hall of Famer.

Rod Carew
Target Field
1 Twins Way
MLB Hall of Famer.

Sharon Sayles Belton
Minneapolis City Hall
350 S. 5th Street
*First woman and African
American mayor of
Minneapolis.*

SHAFER

Tuskegee Airmen
Franconia Sculpture Park
29836 St. Croix Trail
*First black servicemen to serve
as military aviators in the U.S.
armed forces.*

ST. PAUL

Frank Boyd
Frank Boyd Park
335 Selby Avenue
*Pullman Porter and organizer
of the St. Paul Brotherhood of
Sleeping Car Porters Union.*

MISSISSIPPI

BATESVILLE

**Martin Luther King, Jr. &
Thich Nhat Hanh**
123 Towles Road
*Thich Nhat Hanh and Dr.
Martin Luther King Jr. met for
the first time in 1966 to discuss
civil rights, freedom and peace.*

COLUMBIA

Walter Payton
Walter Payton Field
Gardner Stadium
1009 Broad Street
NFL Hall of Famer.

CORINTH

Corinth Contraband Camp
902 N. Parkway Street
*African Americans who fled
Southern plantations and
farms seeking freedom and
protection, found the Union-
occupied Corinth to be a
secure location.*

HATTIESBURG

Vernon Dahmer
Forrest County Courthouse
700 N. Main Street
*Civil rights activist who
was murdered by the White
Knights of the Ku Klux
Klan for recruiting African
Americans to vote.*

INDIANOLA

B.B. King
B.B. King Park
714 W. Detroit Avenue
*King's signature guitar is
named Lucille.*

JACKSON

James Hill
Mount Olive Cemetery
John R. Lynch Street &
Short Street
*Mississippi's secretary of state
from 1874-1878.*

Medgar Evers
Medgar Evers Library
4215 Medgar
Evers Boulevard
*Assassinated June 12, 1963
in front of his driveway in
Jackson, MS.*

Richard Wright
Lamar Street &
Capitol Street
Writer and poet.

LORMAN

Medgar Evers
Alcorn State University
1000 Asu Drive
*NAACP Secretary and civil
rights activist.*

OXFORD

James Meredith
The University of
Mississippi
University Avenue
First African American

*student at the University of
Mississippi.*

RULEVILLE

Fannie Lou Hamer
726 Byron Street
*Voting rights activist and civil
rights leader.*

VICKSBURG

**African
American Monument**
3201 Clay Street
*Commemorating the Service
of the 1st and 3d Mississippi
Infantry, African Descent and
All Mississippians of African
Descent Who Participated in
the Vicksburg Campaign."*

WEST POINT

Howlin' Wolf
Howlin Wolf Blues Museum
307 E. Westbrook Street
Blues singer.

MISSOURI

BOONVILLE

James Milton Turner
Morgan Street Park
Main Street & Morgan Street
Ex-slave and educator.

BUTLER

1st Kansas Colored Infantry
Civil War Monument
7 W. Ohio Street
*Commemorates the role
of the 1st Kansas in the In
October 29, 1862, Skirmish
at Island Mound in Bates
County, Missouri.*

DIAMOND

Boy Carver
George Washington Carver
National Monument
5646 Carver Road
*Carver appeared on the U.S.
commemorative postal stamp
in 1948 and 1998.*

George Washington Carver
George Washington Carver
National Monument
5646 Carver Road
*The Missouri Botanical Garden
opened the George Washington*

*Carver Garden in 2005 in St.
Louis, MO.*

JEFFERSON CITY

Soldiers' Memorial
Lincoln University
820 Chestnut Street
*Commemorates the 62nd
and 65th United States
Colored Infantry.*

KANSAS CITY

Charlie Parker
Charlie Parker
Memorial Plaza
17th Terrace & the
Paseo Boulevard
Jazz saxophonist and composer.

Dr. John Williams
The Paseo & Truman Road
*Civil rights activist and pastor
of St. Stephen Baptist Church.*

Leon M. Jordan
Leon M. Jordan
Memorial Park
31st Street &
Benton Boulevard
*Police officer, politician and
civil rights leader.*

**Negro Baseball
League Players***
Negro Leagues

Baseball Museum
1616 E. 18th Street
*History of the Negro League
Baseball Players.*

ST. CHARLES

Lou Brock
Lou Brock Sports Complex
Lindenwood University
209 S. Kingshighway Street
MLB Hall of Famer.

ST. LOUIS

Bob Gibson
Busch Gardens
8th Street & Clark Avenue
MLB Hall of Famer.

Frankie Muse Freeman, Esq.
Kiener Plaza
500 Chestnut Street
Civil rights attorney.

Harriet & Dred Scott
Old Courthouse
4th Street & Market Street
*Dred Scott unsuccessfully sued
for his freedom and that of his
wife and their two daughters
in the Dred Scott v. Sandford
case of 1857.*

James "Popa Cool" Bell
Busch Stadium

8th Street & Clark Avenue
MLB Hall of Famer.

Lou Brock
Busch Stadium
8th Street & Clark Avenue
MLB Hall of Famer.

Martin Luther King, Jr.
Fountain Park
Fountain Avenue &
Aubert Avenue
*King was born
Michael King, Jr.*

Ozzie Smith
Busch Stadium
8th Street & Clark Avenue
MLB Hall of Famer.

UNIVERSITY CITY

Chuck Berry
Melville Avenue &
Delmar Boulevard
Pioneer of rock and roll music.

WARRENSBURG

John William Boone
402 W. Pine Street
Blind pianist and composer.

NEBRASKA

OMAHA

Jazz Trio
Dreamland Park
24th & Lizzie
Robinson Drive
Jazz trio performing on stage.

Marlin Briscoe*
University of Nebraska
Baxter Arena
2425 S. 67th Street
*First African American
quarterback of the NFL.*

Martin Luther King, Jr.
Douglas County Courthouse
Civic Plaza
1701 Farnam Street
*King was born on
January 15, 1929.*

Michael P. Anderson
Creighton University
Hixon-Lied Science Building
2500 California Plaza
*Space Shuttle Columbia
Astronaut.*

Mildred Brown
Mildred Brown
Strolling Park
24th & Grant Street
Journalist and civil
rights activist.

PAPILLION

Bob Gibson
Werner Park
12356 Ballpark Way
MLB Hall of Famer.

NEVADA

LAS VEGAS

Martin Luther King, Jr.
1344 W. Carey Avenue
*Martin Luther King, Jr.
Boulevard & Carey Avenue
King was the middle child of
Michael King, Sr. and Alberta
Williams King.*

NEW HAMPSHIRE

MILFORD

Harriet Wilson
Clinton Street & South Street
*First African American woman
to publish a novel in the
United States.*

PORTSMOUTH

African Burial Grounds
Chestnut Street between
Court & State Street
The separation, uncertainty,

difficulty, and perseverance experienced by those individuals brought to this country as captives.

NEW JERSEY

ATLANTIC CITY

Arfien Clifford Ali
All Wars Memorial Building
Adriatic Avenue & New York Avenue
First city resident killed in the Vietnam War.

Leavander Johnson
Center City Park
1222 Atlantic Avenue
Lightweight boxer.

William C. Walker Jr.
All Wars Memorial Building
Adriatic Avenue & New York Avenue
Tuskegee Airmen.

CAMDEN

Charles Barkley
76ers Training Facility
76ers Legends Walk
1-99 S. Front Street
NBA Fall of Famer.

Hal Greer
76ers Training Facility

76ers Legends Walk
1-99 S. Front Street
NBA Hall of Famer.

Julius Erving
76ers Training Facility
76ers Legends Walk
1-99 S. Front Street
NBA Hall of Famer.

Matthew Henson
Camden Shipyard and Maritime Museum
1912 S. Broadway
African American explorer *best known as the co-discoverer of the North Pole.*

Maurice Cheeks
76ers Training Facility
76ers Legends Walk
1-99 S. Front Street
NBA Hall of Famer.

Wilt Chamberlain
76ers Training Facility
76ers Legends Walk
1-99 S. Front Street
NBA Hall of Famer.

JERSEY CITY

Jackie Robinson
Journal Square
138 Magnolia Avenue
Robinson was the first African American Vice President at Chock Full O' Nuts.

NEWARK

Althea Gibson
Branch Brook Park
Lake Street & Park Avenue
*First African American tennis
player to compete at the U.S.
National Championships
in 1950, and the first
black player to compete at
Wimbledon in 1951.*

Donald Payne
Essex County
Government Complex
50 W. Market Street
*First black legislator in the
United States Congress.*

Martin Luther King, Jr.
Essex County Hall
of Records
MLK Boulevard &
Springfield Avenue
*King's grandfather A.D.
Williams was a minister.*

Rosa Parks
Essex County
Government Complex
Veterans Courthouse
50 W. Market Street
*Parks married her husband
Raymond Parks on
December 18, 1932.*

PATERSON

**Huntoon-Van Rensalier
Underground Railroad**
Broadway &
Memorial Drive
*A white man Josiah Huntoon,
and a former black slave
William Van Rensalier,
manned secret routes and safe
houses to assist escaping slaves
on their journey north.*

TEANECK

Martin Luther King, Jr.
Fairleigh Dickinson
University
1000 River Road
*King had an older sister, Willie
Christine.*

NEW MEXICO

ALBUQUERQUE

Brent Woods
New Mexico
Veterans Memorial
1100 Louisiana
Boulevard, SE
Buffalo Soldier.

Cpl. Clinton Greaves
Fort Bayard Memorial
Buffalo Soldier Road &

Forsythe Road
Buffalo Soldier.

Tuskegee Airmen
1100 Louisiana
Boulevard, SE
*First black servicemen to serve
as military aviators in the U.S.
armed forces.*

RADIUM SPRINGS

Buffalo Soldier
Ft. Selden State Monument
1280 Fort Selden Road
*Instrumental in establishing
territory which would later
become New Mexico.*

NEW YORK

ALBANY

Henry Johnson
Willett Street &
Madison Street
World War I Hero.

Martin Luther King, Jr.
Lincoln Park
Eagle Street &
Morton Avenue
*King had a younger brother,
Alfred Daniel William King.*

AUBURN

Harriet Tubman
25 S. Street
*Harriet Tubman assisted the
Union Army as a spy, cook,
nurse and guide.*

BINGHAMPTON

Martin Luther King, Jr.
Binghampton River Walk
Wall Street &
Morton Avenue
*"We know through painful
experience that freedom is
never voluntarily given by the
oppressor. It must be demanded
by the oppressed." – Letter
from Birmingham Jail.*

BUFFALO

Martin Luther King, Jr.
Martin Luther King, Jr. Park
84 Parkside Avenue
*In 1954, King became a
pastor to Dexter Avenue
Baptist Church.*

COOPERSTOWN

Jackie Robinson
National Baseball Hall of
Fame and Museum
25 Main Street

Robinson portrayed himself in the movie "The Jackie Robinson Story."

Satchel Paige
National Baseball Hall of Fame and Museum
25 Main Street, South Lawn
Negro League and Major League Baseball pitcher.

ELMIRA

Ernie Davis
Ernie Davis Academy
933 Hoffman Street
First African American to win the Heisman Trophy.

FLUSHING

Althea Gibson
Arthur Ashe Stadium
Billie Jean King National Tennis Center
124-02 Roosevelt Avenue
First African American tennis player to compete at the U.S. National Championships in 1950, and the first black player to compete at Wimbledon in 1951.

HEMPSTEAD

Frederick Douglass
Hofstra University
Frederick Douglass Circle
Daniel L. Monroe Center
1000 Fulton Avenue
Human rights leader in the anti-slavery movement and the first African American citizen to hold a high U.S. government rank.

HIGHLAND

Sojourner Truth
Hudson State Park Westside
87 Haviland Road
"If the first woman God ever made was strong enough to turn the world upside down all alone, these women together ought to be able to turn it back, and get it right side up again! And now they is asking to do it, the men better let them."

LEWISTON

Freedom Crossing Monument
North Water Street & Center Street
Runaway slaves on the last leg of their journey

to freedom along the
Underground Railroad.

NEW YORK CITY

Adam Clayton Powell, Jr.
125th Street & Adam
Clayton Powell Jr. Boulevard
First African American elected
to the New York City Council.

Benjamin Lowry
523 Washington Avenue
Washington Avenue near
Atlantic Avenue
Long-time pastor of Zion
Baptist Church.

Clara Hale
Hale House Center, Inc.
152 W. 122nd Street
Nurtured hundreds
of abandoned and
orphaned babies.

Countee Cullen*
Countee Cullen
Public Library
104 W. 136 Street
Poet, novelist & playwright.

Duke Ellington
110th Street & Fifth Avenue
Pianist, jazz-band leader,
and composer of over 2,000
pieces of music.

Frederick Douglass
110th Street &

Eighth Avenue
Human rights leader in the
anti-slavery movement and
the first African American
citizen to hold a high U.S.
government rank.

Friends
120th Street & 5th Avenue
Three voluptuous women
sitting together and
hanging out.

Gabby Douglas
1285 Avenue of the Americas
Olympic gymnast and the
first African American
to win the individual all-
around event. She won gold
medals at the 2012 and 2016
Summer Olympics.

Harriet Tubman
St. Nicholas
Avenue & Frederick
Douglass Boulevard
In 1869, Harriet Tubman
married her second husband
Nelson Davis.

**Jackie Robinson and
Pee Wee Reese**
Coney Island Beach
& Boardwalk
Representative of a time in
history, beyond baseball, that
in the late 1940s reached to the
deepest, the most tragic, and

yet the most elevating moments of a nation in racial crisis.

Lincoln and Boy
Abraham Lincoln
Housing Projects
135th Street &
Madison Avenue
President Lincoln and newly freed black youth.

Malcolm X*
Audubon Ballroom
3940 Broadway
Muslim minister and human rights activist.

Martin Luther King, Jr.
Esplanade Gardens
Between 147th & 151st along the Harlem River.
Minister & civil rights leader.

Monumental Women
Central Park
Sojourner Truth, Susan B. Anthony and Elizabeth Cady Stanton.

Nelson Mandela*
United Nations
Headquarters in New York
46th Street & 1st Avenue
Former President of South Africa.

Oprah Winfrey
1285 Avenue of the Americas
Television personality, actress, and entrepreneur.

Peter and Willie
Imagination Playground
Ocean Avenue &
Lincoln Road
Peter and his dachshund, Willie—familiar characters in the stories of best-selling children's book, Peter's Chair.

Ralph Ellison
Invisible Man
Riverside Park at
150th Street
Writer and scholar.

Ronald McNair
Ronald McNair Park
Union Street &
Classon Avenue
Physicist and astronaut Ronald McNair, who died aboard the Challenger space shuttle when it exploded in 1986.

Soul in Flight – A Memorial to Arthur Ashe
Arthur Ashe Stadium
124-02 Roosevelt Avenue
Flushing Meadows-
Corona Park.
Ashe was born on July 10, 1943, in Richmond, VA.

Tererai Trent
1285 Avenue of the Americas
Educator, mentor and motivational speaker, and founder of Tererai Trent International (TTI).

LIST OF MONUMENTAL STATUES & MONUMENTS

PORT EWEN

The Child Who Became Sojourner Truth
Sojourner Truth Memorial
9W & Salem Street
Sojourner Truth was sold for $100 at a slave auction.

ROCHESTER

Frederick Douglass
Corinthian Street & State Street
Site of Douglass' renowned Fourth of July speech.

Frederick Douglass
Central Avenue & St. Paul Street
He chose to celebrate his birthday on February 14.

Frederick Douglass
Hochstein School of Music and Dance
50 Plymouth Avenue North
Formerly the Central Presbyterian Church where Douglass was funeralized.

Frederick Douglass
30 Alexander Street
Douglass' first home.

Frederick Douglass
Highland Park
Robinson Drive &

South Avenue
Human rights leader in the anti-slavery movement and the first African American citizen to hold a high U.S. government rank.

Frederick Douglass
Hope Cemetery
1133 Mt Hope Avenue
Douglass family's burial site.

Frederick Douglass
Maplewood Park
Kelsey's Landing
(departure point for the Underground Railroad)
89 Maplewood Drive
Direct slaves to freedom at this location.

Frederick Douglass
North Star Publishing
Talman Building
25 E. Main Street
The Frederick Douglass Newspaper and The North Star was published at this location.

Frederick Douglass
42 Favor Street
Original site of North Star Press and a stop on the Underground Railroad.

Frederick Douglass
Rochester Educational Opportunity Center
161 Chestnut Street –
Main Entrance

Wrote his autobiography, Narrative of the Life of Frederick Douglass.

Frederick Douglass
Seward School
Alexander Street &
Tracy Street.
Site of the school where Douglass' children attended.

Frederick Douglass
999 South Avenue
Site of Frederick Douglass Family Farm

Frederick Douglass*
University of Rochester
Rush Rees Library
55 Library Road
Douglass lived in Rochester from 1847 to 1872.

Frederick Douglass
Washington Square Park
10 St. Mary's Place
Douglass was the most photographed American of the 19th century.

Let's Have Tea
Susan B. Anthony Park
Madison Street &
King Street
Frederick Douglass and Susan B. Anthony having tea while peering over two books, resting on a table which stands in the middle of the two.

SYRACUSE

Eric Dolphy
LeMoyne College
1419 Salt Springs Road
Dablon Quad
Jazz alto saxophonist.

Ernie Davis
The Plaza 44
Syracuse University
Ensley Athletic Center
First African American to win the Heisman Trophy.

Floyd Little
The Plaza 44
Syracuse University
Ensley Athletic Center
NFL Hall of Famer.

Jerry Rescue
Clinton Street & Water Street
William Henry, an escaped slave who was living in Syracuse as Jerry McReynolds was arrested under the Fugitive Slave Act of 1850. On October 1, 1851, a group of citizens helped "Jerry" escape from jail and getaway to Canada.

Jim Brown
The Plaza 44
Syracuse University
Ensley Athletic Center
NFL Hall of Famer.

WHITE PLAINS

Martin Luther King, Jr.
Westchester County
Courthouse
111 Dr. Martin Luther King,
Jr. Boulevard
In 1966, gave a speech at
Soldier Field in Chicago.

YONKERS

Ella Fitzgerald
Metro-North Station
Buena Vista Avenue &
Main Street
The First Lady of Jazz.

NORTH CAROLINA

ASHEVILLE

Martin Luther King, Jr.
Martin Luther King, Jr. Park
50 Martin Luther
King, Jr. Drive
Dr. Martin Luther King, Jr.
eulogized the funerals of Addie
Mae Collins, Carol Denise
McNair, and Cynthia Wesley
who were victims of the 16th
Street Baptist Church bombing.

CHAPEL HILL

The Student Body
University of North Carolina
Hamilton Hall &
Manning Hall
African American man
spinning a basketball on his
finger, an African American
woman balancing a book
on her head.

Unsung
Founders Memorial
University of North Carolina
McCorkle Place
African Americans who helped
build North Carolina.

CHARLOTTE

Martin Luther King, Jr.
Marshall Park
800 E. 3rd Street
"America has given the
Negro people a bad check
which has come back marked
insufficient funds." – I Have A
Dream speech.

Sam Mills
Bank of America Stadium
800 S. Mint Street
North entrance
NFL Player with the North
Carolina Panthers.

Thaddeus Lincoln Tate
Uptown Charlotte near the
Metropolitan on the Little
Sugar Creek Greenway.
*Barbershop owner and
civic leader.*

Transportation
Trade Street & Tryon Street
*African American man
representing the builders of the
very first railroads in Charlotte.*

DURHAM

James Shepard
North Carolina Central
University
1801 Fayetteville Street
Front of the Hoey
Administration Building
*Founder of North Carolina
College for Negroes in Durham
that is now North Carolina
Central University.*

ELIZABETH CITY

Seat of Knowledge
Elizabeth City State
University
Griffin Hall
1704 Weeksville Road
*Depicting President-Emeritus
Peter W. Moore.*

FAYETTEVILLE

Martin Luther King, Jr.
MLK Memorial Park
739 Blue Street
*Martin Luther King, Jr. was
stabbed in the chest with
a letter opener by Izola
Curry in 1958.*

GREENSBORO

February One
1601 E. Market Street
*Four AT&T college freshman
students walked into a
Woolworth segregated lunch
counter in 1960 that sparked
lunch counter sit-ins around
the United States.*

George Simkins Jr.
Old Guilford County
Courthouse
201 S. Eugene Street
Dentist and civil rights activist.

Greensboro Four
North Carolina A&T State
University
1601 E. Market Street
*Four AT&T college freshman
students walked into a
Woolworth segregated lunch
counter in 1960 that sparked
lunch counter sit-ins around
the United States.*

Jimmie I. Barber
Barber Park
1500 Barber Park Drive
Former Greensboro city
councilman.

Life's Journey
Weatherspoon Art Museum
Sculpture Garden
Spring Garden Street &
Tate Street
Journeys made by so many
African Americans in
Greensboro.

Martin Luther King, Jr.
501 S. Elm Street,
Corner of Martin Luther
King, Jr. Drive & S.
Elm Street
King stayed in Room 30
which was used as a "war
room" at the Gaston Motel in
Birmingham, AL.

Paul Robeson
North Carolina A&T
University
Paul Robeson Theater
1601 E. Market Street
Athlete, singer, actor, and
advocate for civil rights.

Ron McNair
North Carolina A&T
University
McNair Hall
1601 E. Market Street
Physicist and astronaut,

Ronald McNair, who died
aboard the Challenger
space shuttle when it
exploded in 1986.

HIGH POINT

John Coltrane
Commerce Avenue &
Hamilton Street
Legendary jazz saxophonist.

John Coltrane
High Point University
1 University Parkway
Kester
International Promenade
Coltrane was born on
September 23, 1926, in
Hamlet, NC.

Martin Luther King, Jr.
High Point University
1 University Parkway
Qubein School of
Communications
Book: The Radical King by
Cornel West.

Maya Angelou
High Point University
1 University Parkway
Caine Conservatory
Poet, writer and activist.

Rosa Parks
High Point University
1 University Parkway

Kester
International Promenade
Parks received over forty-three honorary doctorate degrees.

MANTEO

Richard Etheridge
Traffic circle at Bideford Street & Sir Walter Raleigh Street
First African American United States Life-Saving Service Keeper at Pea Island Station.

RALEIGH

Martin Luther King, Jr.
Dr. Martin Luther King, Jr. Memorial Gardens
900 Rock Quarry Road
Intersection of Martin Luther King Boulevard & Rock Quarry Road
Book: April 4, 1968, by Michael Eric Dyson.

Thomas Day
North Carolina Museum of History
5 E. Edenton Street
Furniture and cabinet maker of the antebellum period.

ROCKY MOUNT

Martin Luther King, Jr.
Martin Luther King, Jr. Park
800 E. Virginia Street
Children's Book: My Daddy Dr. Martin Luther King, Jr. by Martin Luther King III.

TYRON

Nina Simone
Nina Simone Plaza
54 Trade Street
Singer, songwriter, pianist, arranger, and civil rights activist.

WINSTON-SALEM

George Henry Black
Second Street & Chestnut Street
Master brickmaker.

Simon Green Atkins
Winston-Salem State University
CG O'Kelly Library
601 S. Martin Luther King, Jr. Drive
Founder and president of Winston-Salem State University and North Carolina Negro Teacher's Association.

OHIO

ADA

Martin Luther King, Jr.
Ohio Northern University
525 S Main Street
"Out of the mountain of despair, a stone of hope."

BEREA

Harrison Dillard
Baldwin Wallace University
George Finnie Stadium
141 E. Bagley Road
*Four-time Olympic
gold medalist.*

CINCINNATI

Joe Morgan
Great American Ball Park
100 Joe Nuxhall Way
Joe Nuxhall & Johnny
Bench Ways
MLB Hall of Famer.

Oscar Robertson
Fifth Third Arena
2700 O'Varsity Way
NBA Hall of Famer.

CLEVELAND

Frank Robinson
Progressive Field
Heritage Park
9th Street & Eagle Street
*First African American MLB
Outfielder and Manager*

Jesse Owens
Fort Huntington Park
3rd Street & Lakeside Street
*Owens was born on September
12, 1913, in Oakville, AL.*

Jim Brown
FirstEnergy Stadium
100 Alfred Lerner Way
*Brown was born on
February 17, 1936.*

Larry Doby
Progressive Field
9th Street & Eagle Street
*First African American player
in the American League.*

Soldier & Sailors
3 Public Square
*A section of the monument is
a black soldier takes an oath of
allegiance to the United States
and Abraham Lincoln offers
him freedom and a rifle.*

Stephanie Tubbs Jones
108th Street &
East Boulevard

Ohio's first African American Congresswoman.

Stephanie Tubbs Jones
RTA Transit Center
2110 Prospect Avenue
Born on September 10, 1949 in Cleveland, OH.

COLUMBUS

Elijah Pierce
Columbus State
Community College
Long Street &
Washington Street
Woodcarver, barber and minister.

Jesse Owens
Ohio State University
Jesse Owens
Memorial Stadium
2450 Fred Taylor Drive
Owens died on March 31, 1980.

DAYTON

Martin Luther King, Jr.
University of Dayton
300 College Park
"True peace is not merely the absence of tension; it is the presence of justice."

MANSFIELD

Martin Luther King, Jr.
Manfield's Central Park
29 Park Avenue E
"The ultimate measure of a man is not where he stands in moments of comfort and convenience, but where he stands at times of challenge and controversy."

OBERLIN

Martin Luther King, Jr.
Martin Luther King, Jr. Park
17 E Vine Street
"Intelligence plus character — that is the goal of true education."

SANDUSKY

Path to Freedom
Facer Park
Hancock Street &
Shoreline Drive
Slave family's (man, woman, and child) flight to freedom.

TOLEDO

Martin Luther King, Jr.
Martin Luther King Bridge
Children's book: March

On!: The Day My Brother Martin Changed the World by Christine King Farris.

WILBERFORCE

Paul Robeson
Central State University
Administrative Building
1400 Brush Row Road
Robeson graduated from Rutgers in 1919.

OKLAHOMA

LANGSTON

Ernest L. Holloway
Langston University
701 Sammy Davis Jr. Drive
Longest-serving president of Langston University.

John Mercer Langston
Langston University
701 Sammy Davis Jr. Drive
Abolitionist, lawyer, politician and public speaker.

LAWTON

Buffalo Solider
Heritage Plaza
2nd Street & Gore Boulevard
African American cavalry

regiments of the U.S. Army who served in the western United States from 1867 to 1896, mainly fighting Indians on the frontier.

OKLAHOMA CITY

Charles B. Hall
Tinker Air Force Base
3001 S. Douglas Boulevard
Tuskegee Airmen.

Wilbur Joe Rogan
RedHawks Ballpark
2 S. Mickey Mantle Drive
Negro Baseball League Player.

STILLWATER

Nancy Randolph Davis
Oklahoma State University
Human Sciences Building
First African American to attend Oklahoma A&M College.

TULSA

Ellis Walker Woods
Greenwood Avenue & John Hope Franklin Boulevard
Founding principal of Tulsa's first black high school during segregation.

Hope
John Hope Franklin
Reconciliation Park
Hope Plaza
321 N. Detroit Avenue
A white Red Cross worker cradling a black child.

Hostility
John Hope Franklin
Reconciliation Park
Hope Plaza
321 N. Detroit Avenue
An armed white man.

Humiliation
John Hope Franklin
Reconciliation Park
Hope Plaza
321 N. Detroit Avenue
A black man arms raised in surrender.

Tower of Reconciliation
John Hope Franklin
Reconciliation Park
321 N. Detroit Avenue
Memorializing the history of the 1921 Tulsa Race Riot.

OREGON

EUGENE

Rosa Parks
Rosa Parks Plaza
Lane Transit District
3500 E. 17th Avenue

Parks received the Medal of Freedom Award in 1996.

PORTLAND

Martin Luther King, Jr.
The Dream
Oregon Convention Center
777 NE Martin Luther King, Jr. Boulevard
Book: My Life with Martin Luther King, Jr. by Coretta Scott King.

York: Terra Incognita
Lewis & Clark College
615 S. Palatine Hill Road
Slave and explorer with Lewis & Clark.

PENNSYLVANIA

ALLENTOWN

Martin Luther King, Jr. & Coretta Scott King
Harry A. Roberts Plaza
Martin Luther King, Jr. Drive & Union Street
Civil rights leaders.

BRISTOL

Harriet Tubman
Basin Park

Near Otter Creek &
Delaware River
*A reward for the capture
of Harriet Tubman was
estimated $40,000.*

CHESTER

Martin Luther King, Jr.
Martin Luther King Jr.
Memorial Park
6th Street & Engle Street
*Book: Where Do We Go From
Here by Martin Luther King, Jr.*

EASTON

Larry Holmes
128 Larry Holmes Drive
Professional boxer.

LEWISBURG

Edward McKnight Brawley
Bucknell University
1 Dent Drive
Vaughn Literature Building
*First African American student
to attend Bucknell University.*

PHILADELPHIA

**All Wars Memorial
to Colored Soldiers**

and Sailors
Benjamin Franklin Parkway
& 20th Street
*Commemorate the heroism and
sacrifice of all colored soldiers
who served in the various
wars engaged in by the United
States of America.*

Joe Frazier
Xfinity Live
1100 Pattison Avenue
*World heavyweight boxing
champion from February 1970
until January 1973.*

Julius Erving
Wells Fargo Stadium
3601 S. Broad Street
NBA Hall of Famer.

MVP
Smith Playground
2100 S. 24th St.
*Young teenage girl holding
a basketball was inspired by
the legendary athlete, Ora
Washington.*

Octavius V. Catto
Philadelphia City Hall
Broad Street & South
Penn Square
*Educator and Civil
Rights Activist.*

Philadelphia Stars
The Philadelphia
Stars Negro League
Memorial Park

Belmont Avenue &
Parkside Avenue
Negro League.

Richard Allen
Mother Bethel African
Methodist Episcopal Church
419 S. 6th Street
Richard T. Allen Avenue &
Lombard Avenue
Methodist minister and
founder the African Methodist
Episcopal Church.

Wilt Chamberlain
Wells Fargo Stadium
3601 S. Broad Street
NBA Hall of Famer.

PITTSBURGH

Josh Gibson*
Heinz History Center
1212 Smallman Street
Negro league baseball catcher.

Willie Stargill
PNC Park
Federal Street &
Isabella Street
MLB Hall of Famer.

RADNOR

Emlen Tunnell
Radnor Township
Municipal Building

301 Iven Avenue
First African American to play
for the New York Giants, NFL
scout and assistant coach and
Hall of Famer.

WEST CHESTER

Frederick Douglass
West Chester University
700 S. High Street
Human rights leader in the
anti-slavery movement and
the first African American
citizen to hold a high U.S.
government rank.

SOUTH CAROLINA

ANDERSON

Cpl. Freddie Stowers
Anderson University
316 Boulevard
During World War I, Stowers
was hit with machine gun
fire but continued crawling
towards the enemy until being
hit a second time. Stowers
urged his unit to continue
before dying of his wounds, and
the inspired men successfully
forced the Germans off the hill
and into retreat.

James "Radio" Kennedy
T.L. Hanna High School
2600 N. Highway 81
Near Football
Field Bleachers
*Mentally disabled and mascot
at T.L. Hanna High School that
carried a transistor radio that
he kept in his pocket. A 2003
movie was based on his story
called "Radio."*

BEAUFORT

Harriet Tubman
911 Craven Street
*Harriet Tubman made an
estimate of 19 trips to help
fugitive slaves to freedom.*

Robert Smalls
907 Craven Street
*Born into slavery who became
a U.S. Congressman in
South Carolina.*

CAMDEN

Reconciliation
City of Camden
Laurens Court & and
Dekalb Street
*African American baseball
legend Larry Doby and Jewish
financier and presidential
adviser Bernard Baruch.*

CHARLESTON

Denmark Vesey
Hampton Park
30 Mary Murray Drive
*Founder of Emanuel A.M.E.
Church who attempted to lead
a slave rebellion in Charleston.*

Philip Simmons
Hampstead Square
67 Columbus Street
*Artisan and blacksmith
specializing in the craft
of ironwork.*

CHERAW

Dizzy Gillespie
321 Market Street
Between Market Street &
2nd Avenue
Jazz trumpeter.

COLUMBIA

**African American
History Monument**
1100 Gervais Street
Located on Sumter Street
*Traces African American
history from the Middle
Passage, to the fight for freedom
in the Civil War, the struggle
for civil rights and emergence
into mainstream America.*

George Rogers
Williams-Brice Stadium
Bluff Road & George
Rogers Boulevard
NFL Hall of Famer.

Richard T. Greener
University of South Carolina
Thomas Cooper Library
1322 Greene Street
*First African American
graduate of Harvard
University.*

Matthew J. Perry, Jr.
Honorable Matthew J Perry
Federal Courthouse
901 Richland Street
*Civil rights pioneer and
South Carolina's first African
American United States
District Judge.*

FLORENCE

Dr. R.N. Beck
Francis Marion University
Irby Street & Evans Street
Physician and humanitarian.

William H. Johnson
West Evans
Street Breezeway
*Artist that depict the life of
African Americans during the
1930s and 1940s.*

FOUNTAIN INN

Peg Leg Bates
Fairview Street &
Main Street
One-legged tap dancer.

GREENVILLE

Peg Leg Bates
Washington Street &
Spring Street
*Bates lost his leg due to a
cotton mill accident.*

Two Sterling High
School Students
Main Street &
Washington Street
*Students of Greenville's black
high school who's protests
and sit-ins helped bring about
racial integration in 1970.*

GREENWOOD

Benjamin Mays
Dr. Benjamin E. Mays
Historical
Preservation Site
237 N Hospital Street
*Educator and civil
rights activist.*

LAKE CITY

Huey Cooper & His Lucky Rabbits Foot
Acline Street & Main Street
A fixture in the community, would hang out in downtown Lake City and encourage passers-by to rub his lucky rabbit's foot for a nickel.

Ron McNair
Ron McNair Memorial Park
221 E. Main Street
Physicist and astronaut Ronald McNair, who died aboard the Challenger space shuttle when it exploded in 1986.

MOUNT PLEASANT

Willowing Hands
1164 Oakland Market Road
Preservation of the Sweetgrass basket weavers.

SPARTANBURG

Marian Anderson
Converse College
580 East Main Street
Famous contralto and civil rights activist.

WATERLOO

Tuskegee Airmen
537 Aviation Way
African American military pilots (fighter and bomber) who fought in World War II.

SOUTH DAKOTA

RAPID CITY

Barack Obama
4th Street & St. Joseph Street
44th President of the United States.

TENNESSEE

CLARKSVILLE

Wilma Rudolph
Wilma Rudolph
Event Center
1190 Cumberland Drive
First American woman to win three gold medals at a single Olympics in 1960, at the Summer Games in Rome.

CLINTON

The Clinton 12
101 School Street
First students to desegregate

a state-supported high school in the south. They also gave Clinton High School the honor of graduating the first black student from a southern public high school.

KNOXVILLE

Alex Haley
Alex Haley Heritage Square
1620 Dandridge Avenue
Haley was born on August 11, 1921, in Ithaca, NY.

MADISON

United States Colored Troops National Monument
Nashville
National Cemetery
1420 Gallatin Road, S
Section J
In memory of the 20,133 who served as United States Colored Troops in the Union Army.

MEMPHIS

B.B. King
B.B. King Elvis Presley
Welcome Center
119 N Riverside Drive

King was born September 16, 1925, in Itta Bena, MS.

Bobby Blue Bland
Main Street & Martin Luther King, Jr. Avenue.
Blues singer.

Little Milton Campbell
421 S. Main Street
Blue singer and guitarist.

Ramesses II
University of Memphis
Highland Street &
Goodletts Street
Son of Seti I and known as "Ramses the Great."

Rosa Parks*
Civil Rights Museum
450 Mulberry Street
The State of Michigan designated the first Monday following February 4 as Mrs. Rosa Parks' Day.

Tom Lee
Tom Lee Park
Memphis Riverfront & S. Riverside Drive.
Saved the lives of 32 people from a capsized riverboat and was deemed a "Worthy Negro."

W.C. Handy
Handy Park
200 Beale Street
Blues composer and musician.

Willie Herenton
Walker Street &
Neptune Street
*First African American mayor
of Memphis.*

NASHVILLE

Adolpho Birch
402 2nd Avenue, N
*First African American
prosecutor in Davidson
County, a judge in both general
sessions and trial courts, serve
as a chief judge and the second
African American justice on
the state Supreme Court.*

Ed Temple
First Tennessee Park
19 Jr Gilliam Way
Right Field Entrance
Olympic women's track coach.

Emergence
Hartman Park
2801 Tucker Road
*Face of an African American
woman emerging from the
earth. This face serves as a
symbol of every individual's
story of danger, loss, strength
and determination to push
through the setbacks caused by
both nature and man.*

W.E.B. DuBois
Fisk University

1000 17th Avenue, N
*Activists during the first
half of the 20th century. He
co-founded the NAACP and
supported Pan-Africanism.*

TEXAS

AUSTIN

**African American
History Monument**
Austin State Capitol
1100 Congress Avenue
*Honoring the history of
African Americans in Texas.*

Barbara Jordan
Austin-Bergstrom
International Airport
600 Presidential Boulevard
Baggage Level
*First African American
congresswoman to come from
the deep South and the first
woman ever elected to the
Texas Senate.*

Barbara Jordan
The University of
Texas at Austin
110 Inner Campus Drive
24th Street & Whitis Street
*Jordan as born February 21,
1936, in Houston, TX.*

Earl Campbell
The University of

Texas at Austin
Darrell K Royal-Texas
Memorial Stadium
110 Inner Campus Drive
Gate 1
*Former football player and
1977 Heisman Trophy winner.*

George Washington Carver*
George Washington Carver
Museum, Cultural and
Genealogy Center
1165 Angelina Street
*Carver graduated from
Minneapolis High School in
Minneapolis, KS, in 1880.*

Go Forth
George Washington Carver
Museum, Cultural and
Genealogy Center
1165 Angelina Street
*Depicts a mother (Eternity)
ushering forth her two
children, Today (a girl) and
Tomorrow (a boy).*

**Juneteenth
Memorial Monument**
George Washington Carver
Museum, Cultural and
Genealogy Center
1165 Angelina Street
Behind the Museum
*Minister, freedwoman,
freedman and lawmaker
Commemorate the day in
1865 when African American*
*slaves in Texas learned of
their freedom.*

Martin Luther King, Jr.
The University of
Texas at Austin
110 Inner Campus Drive
East Mall
*Children's book: I've Seen the
Promised Land: The Life of
Dr. Martin Luther King, Jr. by
Walter Dean Myers.*

Ricky Williams
The University of
Texas at Austin
Darrell K Royal-Texas
Memorial Stadium
110 Inner Campus Drive
Gate 1
NFL Player.

CONROE

Annette Gordon-Reed
Conroe's Founders
Plaza Park
205 Metcalf Street
*Pulitzer Prize Winner
in History.*

CROCKETT

Myrtis Dightman
1100 Edmiston Drive
Fannin Avenue &
Camp Street

First African American cowboy to qualify for the National Finals Rodeo.

Sam "Lightnin'" Hopkins
215 S. Third Street
Country blues singer, songwriter and guitarist.

DALLAS

Ernie Banks
Booker T. Washington High School for the Performing and Visual Arts
2501 Flora Street
Banks is buried at Graceland Cemetery in Chicago, IL.

Freedsman Memorial
Freedman Memorial Park
Central Expressway & Calvary Drive
Commemorates the lives of more than 5,000 freed slaves who were buried in a once forgotten cemetery.

Martin Luther King, Jr.
Martin Luther King, Jr. Center
2922 Martin Luther King, Jr. Boulevard
Children's book: My Uncle Martin's Words for America: Martin Luther King, Jr.'s Niece Tells How He Made

a Difference by Angela Farris Watkins.

Rosa Parks
Rosa Parks Plaza
8th Street & Corinth Street
1740 E. 8th Street
Parks is interred at Woodlawn Cemetery in Detroit, MI.

EL PASO

Cpl. John Ross
Buffalo Soldier Road & Forsythe Road
Buffalo Soldier.

FORT WORTH

Bill Pickett
121 E. Exchange Avenue
Exchange Avenue & Rodeo Plaza
Rodeo performer who invented the rodeo sport of bulldogging, now known as steer wrestling, and entertained millions of people around the world with his riding and roping skills.

GALVESTON

Jack Johnson
2627 Avenue, M
First African American world heavyweight boxing champion.

HAWKINS

Lenora Rolla
Jarvis Christian College
80 E, Hawkins, TX 75765
*Founder of the Tarrant
County Black Historical and
Genealogical Society.*

HOUSTON

A Tradition of Music
Texas Southern University
Carroll Harris Simms
Sculpture Plaza
3100 Cleburne Street
*The Carroll Harris Simms
Collection.*

Hakeem Olajuwon
Toyota Center
1510 Polk Street
La Branch Street &
Polk Street
NBA Hall of Famer.

Martin Luther King, Jr.
4530 Bricker Street
*Book: Quotations of Martin
Luther King, Jr. by Martin
Luther King, Jr.*

Martin Luther King, Jr.
MacGregor Park
5225 Calhoun
MLK Boulevard & Old
Spanish Trail
King march in Gage Park in

*Chicago in 1966 to
protest against housing
discrimination.*

Martin Luther King, Jr.
Hermann Park
6001 Fannin Street
*King delivered a speech in 1967
in New York City at Riverside
Church on the war in Vietnam.*

Mickey Leland
Hermann Park
6001 Fannin Street
*U.S. Representative for Texas
18th District.*

The African Queen Mother
Texas Southern University
Carroll Harris Simms
Sculpture Plaza
3100 Cleburne Street
*The Carroll Harris Simms
Collection.*

LUBBOCK

C.B. Stubblefield
108 E. Broadway
Barbecue restaurateur.

Tim Cole
19th Street &
University Avenue
*Died in prison, convicted of a
rape he didn't commit.*

NAVASOTA

Mance Lipscomb
Mance Lipscomb Park
140 N. La Salle Street
Blues singer and guitarist.

SAN ANTONIO

Barbara Jordan
The Henry B. Gonzalez
Convention Center
900 E. Market Street
Hall of Statues
2nd Floor
*Jordan died on
January 17, 1996.*

WACO

Doris Miller
Bledsoe-Miller Park
300 Martin Luther King,
Jr. Boulevard
War World II Hero.

Holt Collier
101 N. University
Parks Drive
Franklin Avenue &
University Parks Drive
Hunter & cowboy.

Robert Griffith, III
Baylor University
McLane Stadium
1001 S. Martin Luther King,
Jr. Boulevard
NFL Player.

UTAH

SALT LAKE CITY

Karl Malone
Vivint Smart Home Arena
301 S. Temple
NBA Hall of Famer.

VIRGINIA

ALEXANDRIA

Edmondson Sisters
1701 Duke Street
*Sisters who gained their
freedom from slavery.*

**The Path of
Thorns and Roses**
Contrabands and
Freedmen's Cemetery
1001 S. Washington Street
*The struggle and flight
of freedom.*

FREDERICKSBURG

James Farmer
University of Mary
Washington
Trinkle Hall

1301 College Avenue
*Principal founder of
the C.O.R.E.*

HAMPTON

Barack Obama
Hampton University
Legacy Park
100 E. Queen Street
*Obama was named Time
Magazine's "Person of the
Year" in 2008.*

Booker T. Washington
Hampton University
100 E. Queen Street
*Educator & Founder of
Tuskegee University.*

Jerome Holland
Hampton University
Legacy Park
100 E. Queen Street
*Ninth president of Hampton
Institute in 1960.*

Martin Luther King, Jr.
Hampton University
Legacy Park
100 E. Queen Street
*"The function of education is to
teach one to think intensively
and to think critically.
Intelligence plus character
– that is the goal of true
education."*

Mary Jackson
Hampton University
Legacy Park
100 E. Queen Street
*Mathematician and aerospace
and NASA's first African
American female engineer.*

Mary Peake
Hampton University
Legacy Park
100 E. Queen Street
*A teacher known for starting a
school for children of formers
lave under what became known
as the Emancipation Oak Tree.*

Rosa Parks
Hampton University
Legacy Park
100 E. Queen Street
*Parks was a seamstress,
life insurance agent and
housekeeper.*

**U.S. Army 1st Lt. Ruppert
L. Sargent**
1 Franklin Street
*First African American
officer to be awarded the
Congressional Medal of Honor
for his heroics at Hau Nghia
Province, Republic of Vietnam
on March 15, 1967.*

William R. Harvey
Hampton University
Legacy Park
100 E. Queen Street

President at Hampton University.

HARDY

Booker T. Washington
Booker T.
Washington National
Historic Monument
12130 Booker T.
Washington Highway
Washington was born on April 5, 1856, in Franklin County, VA.

NEWPORT NEWS

Martin Luther King, Jr.
Martin Luther King, Jr. Plaza
25th Street &
Jefferson Avenue
In 1966, King and his family moved to Chicago in the North Lawndale community to march for better living conditions in the black community.

NORFOLK

Breaking Ground
Norfolk Botanical Gardens
6700 Azalea Garden Road
Commemorates the African American women workers.

West Point Monument
West Point Cemetery
238 E. Princess Anne Road
William H. Carney was the first black Congressional Medal of Honor recipient. His story was inspired in the 1989 movie "Glory," which starred Denzel Washington as Carney.

RICHMOND

Arthur Ashe
Monument Avenue &
Roseneath Road
Tennis player & humanitarian.

Arthur Ashe*
Black History Museum and Cultural Center of Virginia
122 W. Leigh Street
Ashe was the first African American male to win the U.S. Open and Wimbledon singles titles.

Bill "Bojangles" Robinson
Adams Street & Leigh Street
Tap dancer & actor.

Civil Rights Memorial
Virginia State Capitol
1000 Bank Street
Near the entrance to the
Executive Mansion
Barbara Johns, who, when she was sixteen years old, led a student walkout from the

woefully inadequate high
school for African Americans
in Farmville, Virginia.

Elizabeth Keckley
Virginia State Capitol
Capitol Square
Voices from the Garden
1000 Bank Street
*Dressmaker, civil rights activist
and author.*

Maggie Walker
Adams Street & Broad Street
*Civil rights activist and
trailblazing entrepreneur.*

Maggie Walker
Virginia State Capitol
Capitol Square
Voices from the Garden
1000 Bank Street
*Walker was the first African
American woman to own
a bank, St. Luke Penny
Savings Bank.*

Oliver Hill*
Black History Museum and
Cultural Center of Virginia
122 W. Leigh Street
Civil rights attorney.

Rumors of War
200 N. Arthur
Ashe Boulevard
*African American man
with dreadlocks dressed in
contemporary clothing riding a
horse in response to confederate*

statues that line up on
Monument Avenue.

Virginia E. Randolph
Virginia State Capitol
Capitol Square
Voices from the Garden
1000 Bank Street
*Educator and founder of
the Virginia Randolph
Training School.*

ROANOKE

Martin Luther King, Jr.
Martin Luther King,
Jr. Bridge
First Street & Henry Street
*King's closest friend was Rev.
Ralph Abernathy.*

WASHINGTON
SEATTLE

Jimi Hendrix
Broadway & Pine Street
*Guitarist, singer, and
songwriter.*

Ken Griffey, Jr.
Safeco Field
1st Avenue South &Edgar
Martinez Drive South
MLB Hall of Famer.

Michael P. Anderson
Museum of Flight
South 94th Place & East
Marginal Way
*Space Shuttle Columbia
Astronaut.*

WEST VIRGINIA

CHARLESTON

Booker T. Washington
West Virginia
Capitol Complex
1979 State Capitol Complex
West Wing Capitol
Building 1
*Washington was invited to
the White House by President
Theodore Roosevelt causing
an uproar.*

HUNTINGTON

Carter G. Woodson
Carter G. Woodson
9th Avenue & Hal
Greer Boulevard
*Woodson was the founder of
the Association for the Study
of African American Life
and History.*

INSTITUTE

Earl Lloyd*
West Virginia State
University
Walker Convocation Center
Earl Lloyd Lobby
5000 Fairlawn Avenue
NBA Hall of Famer.

Katherine Johnson
West Virginia State
University
Thomas W. Cole,
Jr. Complex
124 Ferrell Hall
NASA mathematician.

TALCOTT

John Henry
John Henry Historical Park
Highway 12 & Highway 3
Near the entrance to the Big
Bend railroad tunnel.
*The strongest and most
powerful man working
the rails.*

WISCONSIN

EAU CLAIRE

Hank Aaron
Hank Aaron Stadium
Carson Park

Carson Park Drive & Half Moon Street
MLB Hall of Famer.

LACROSSE

George Coleman Poage
George Coleman Poage Park
Hood Street & Fifth Street
First African American athlete to win a medal in the Olympic Games, winning two bronze medals at the 1904 games in St. Louis.

MILWAUKEE

Hank Aaron
Miller Park
1 Brewers Way
MLB Hall of Famer.

Martin Luther King, Jr.
King Drive Commons
Freedom Garden
27th & Martin Luther King, Jr. Drive Boulevard
King was baptized in 1936.

Martin Luther King, Jr.
King Heights Apartment
1740 N. Martin Luther King, Jr. Drive
King became a pastor of the Dexter Avenue Baptist Church in Montgomery, AL in 1954.

RACINE

Martin Luther King, Jr.
State Street & Marquette Street
King skipped ninth and eleventh grade and enrolled at Morehouse College at age 15.

WYOMING

CHEYENNE

Vernon J. Baker
McComb Avenue & Randall Avenue
Buffalo Soldier.

*Statue located indoors.

EDUCATIONAL SITES OF INTEREST

Bronzeville Historical Society: Sherry Williams, **Website:** bronzevillehistoricalsociety.wordpress.com, **Facebook:** @BronzevilleHistorical, **Email:** bronzevillehistoricalsociety@gmail.com

Hidden Women: Tammy Denease, **Website:** hiddenwomen. org **Email:** tdcr35@yahoo.com

History Before Us: Frederick D. Murphy, **Website:** historybeforeus.com, **Facebook:** @HistoryBeforeUs, **Twitter:** @HistoryBeforeUs, **Instagram:** @historybeforeus, **Email:** historybeforeus@gmail.com

History Unsung 1619: Frederick Murphy, Tammy Gibson, **Facebook:** @historyunsung1619, **Instagram:** @ historyunsung1619, **Email:** historyunsung@gmail.com, Podbean and iTunes

Interpretive Challenges: Emmanuel Dabney, **Website:** interpretivechallenges.wordpress.com

John Sunday Society: Teníadé Broughton, **Website:** johnsunday. org, **Facebook:** @johnsundaysociety, **Instagram:** @ johnsundaysociety, **Email:** info@ johnsunday.org

Nat Williams-The Plug: Nat Williams | **Facebook:** @ NatWilliams-The Plug, **Instagram:** @natwilliamstheplug

Not Your Momma's History: Cheyney McKnight, **Website:** NotYourMommashistory.com, **Facebook:** @ YourMommasHistory, **Email:** notyourmommashistory@ gmail.com, **YouTube:** NotYourMommasHistory

Our Mammy's: Gaynell Brady, **Website:** ourmammys.com, **Facebook:** @ourmammys, **Instagram:** @ourmammys, **Email:** ourmammys@gmail.com

Sankofa TravelHer: Tammy Gibson, **Website:** sankofatravelher. com, **Facebook:** @SankofaTravelher, **Twitter:** @ SankofaTravelHr, **Instagram:** @sankofatravelher, **Email:** sankofatravelher@yahoo.com, **YouTube:** Sankofa TravelHer

The Black Journey: Black Philadelphia Walking Tour: Raina Yancey, **Facebook:** @theblackjourney, **Instagram:** @theblackjourney, **Email:** blackphiladelphiawalkingtour@gmail.com

The Chronicles of Adam: Dontavious Williams, **Website:** thechroniclesofadam.weebly.com, **Facebook:** @ TheChroniclesofAdam, **Twitter:** @chronicleofadam, **Instagram:** @thechroniclesofadam, **Email:** thechroniclesofadam@outlook.com

The Cooking Gene: Michael Twitty, **Website:** afroculinaria. com, **Facebook:** @thecookinggene, **Instagram:** @ thecookinggene, **Email:** thecookinggenebook@gmail.com

The Slave Dwelling Project: Joseph McGill, Jr., **Website:** slavedwellingproject.org, **Facebook:** @ SlaveDwellingProject, **Instagram:** @slavedwellingproject, **YouTube:** The Slave Dwelling Project, **Email:** slavedwellingproject@gmail.com

WAKART, LLC: Kevin A. Williams, **Website:** artbywak.com, **Instagram:** @artbywak

REFERENCES

Aguilera, J. (2020). *Confederate Statues Are Being Removed Amid Protests Over George Floyd's Death. Here's What to Know.* Time Magazine, https://time.com/5849184/confederate-statues-removed/

American Revolutionary War. (2020). *Major General John Philip Schuyler,* https://www.myrevolutionarywar.com/leaders/schuyler-philip/#

Art Daily (n.d.). *PAFA announces Curator of African American artist John Rhoden's works,* https://artdaily.cc/news/103757/PAFA-announces-Curator-of-African-American-artist-John-Rhoden-s-works#.XxB5jyhKiUk

Associated Press. (2020). *'White Lives Matter' Sprayed On Arthur Ashe Memorial In Virginia.* CBS Baltimore, https://baltimore.cbslocal.com/2020/06/17/white-lives-matter-sprayed-on-arthur-ashe-memorial-in-virginia/

AZ Quotes. (n.d.). *Augusta Savage Quotes,* https://www.azquotes.com/author/47171-Augusta_Savage

AZ Quotes. (n.d.). *Elizabeth Catlett Quotes,* https://www.azquotes.com/author/47174-Elizabeth_Catlett

Bagwell, V. (n.d.). *Vinnie Bagwell Sculpture,* https://www.vinniebagwell.com/

Barrett, C. (2020). *Confederate Monument In Garfield Park Is Being Dismantled.* WFYI, https://www.wfyi.org/news/articles/confederate-monument-in-garfield-park-comes-down

Beckman, A. (2016). *Vandalism On Dockum Sit-In Sculpture Affects Plans For Permanent Memorial.* KMUW, https://

www.kmuw.org/post/vandalism-dockum-sit-sculpture-affects-plans-permanent-memorial

Behind The Big House, https://behindthebighouse.org/

Biography.com. (2020). *Augusta Savage Biography* (1892–1962), https://www.biography.com/artist/augusta-savage

Birnbaum, E. (2018). *New York African-American monument vandalized with racist slur.* The Hill, https://thehill.com/homenews/state-watch/414709-colonial-african-american-monument-vandalized-with-racist-slur-in-new

Blair, E. (2012). *The Strange Story Of The Man Behind 'Strange Fruit',* https://www.npr.org/2012/09/05/158933012/the-strange-story-of-the-man-behind-strange-fruit

Brown, J. (2020). *Confederate monument in downtown Huntsville vandalized.* The Huntsville Item, https://www.itemonline.com/news/confederate-monument-in-downtown-huntsville-vandalized/article_cd459094-ab1c-11ea-ac48-57f48601fef1.html

Bunch III, L. G. (2018). *Putting White Supremacy on a Pedestal.* National Museum of African American History and Culture, https://nmaahc.si.edu/blog-post/putting-white-supremacy-pedestal

CBS Boston. (2020). *Beheaded Christopher Columbus Statue In Boston Will Be Removed From North End Park,* https://boston.cbslocal.com/2020/06/10/christopher-columbus-statue-beheaded-boston-massachusetts/

CBS DFW. (2020). *Texas Ranger Statue Removed At Dallas Love Field,* https://dfw.cbslocal.com/2020/06/04/texas-ranger-statue-removed-dallas-love-field/

Crimmins, P. (2017). *PAFA to look after life's work of late sculptor,* https://whyy.org/articles/pafa-look-lifes-work-late-sculptor/#:~:text=The%20Pennsylvania%20

Academy%20of%20the,to%20build%20the%20 artist's%20legacy.

Cusaac-Smith, T. (2020). *Black History Month: Yonkers woman uses sculpture to chronicle the history of black people.* lohud, https://www.lohud.com/story/news/local/ westchester/yonkers/2020/02/11/yonkers-sculpture-sojourner-truth-walkway-hudson/4599075002/

DiNatale, S. (2016). *Image of Donald Trump hat on USF King statue sparks comments on social media.* Tampa Bay Times, https://www.tampabay.com/news/humaninterest/ image-of-donald-trump-hat-on-usf-king-statue-sparks-comments-on-social/2272671/

Dwyer, C. (2020). *Confederate Monument Being Removed After Birmingham Mayor Vows To "Finish The Job."* NPR, https:// www.npr.org/2020/06/02/867659459/confederate-monument-removed-after-birmingham-mayors-vow-to-finish-the-job

Eady, A. (2020a). *Confederate statue in Hemming Park removed in downtown Jacksonville.* CBS 47, https:// www.actionnewsjax.com/news/local/duval-county/ breaking-confederate-monument-hemming-park-appears-be-its-way-down/56ES27ARXFAPDEGGHCE W5RKRUQ/

Eady, A. (2020b). *Jacksonville mayor: All confederate monuments citywide will be removed.* CBS 472, https://www.actionnewsjax.com/news/ local/duval-county/jacksonville-mayor-all-confederate-monuments-citywide-be-removed/ FG5JM2CYHNAABCQFAK5C5PTCVM/

Equal Justice Initiative. (n.d.). *Lynching in America: Confronting the Legacy of Racial Terror,* https://eji.org/reports/ lynching-in-america/

Equal Justice Initiative. (n.d.). *Racial Violence Erupts in Springfield, Illinois,* https://calendar.eji.org/racial-injustice/aug/14

Freed, T. (2017). *Winter Park war hero Richard Hall, Jr. served with the Tuskegee Airmen.* Orange Observer, https://www.orangeobserver.com/article/winter-park-war-hero-richard-hall-jr-served-with-the-tuskegee-airmen

Freed, T. (2019). *Vandalized Tuskegee Airman statue in Winter Park repaired.* Orange Observer, https://www.orangeobserver.com/article/vandalized-tuskegee-airman-statue-in-winter-park-repaired

Frey, K. (2020). *Sculptures have been part of campus history for 40 years.* PennState Scranton, https://scranton.psu.edu/feature/sculptures-have-been-part-campus-history-40-years

Garcia, S. E. (2020). *Arthur Ashe Statue in Virginia Vandalized With 'White Lives Matter.'* New York Times, https://www.nytimes.com/2020/06/17/us/arthur-ashe-statue-vandalized.html

Gross, R. (2014). *The Influence of Africa on U.S. Culture.* National Endowment for the Arts, https://www.arts.gov/NEARTS/2014v1-opening-world-international-art/influence-africa-us-culture

Hand, D. (n.d.). *About the Artist–Debra Hand,* http://www.handstudios.com/

Hernando Sun. (2018). *The assassination of Judge William Center: one of many murders after reconstruction,* https://www.hernandosun.com/The-assassination-of-Judge-William-Center

Hightower, F. (n.d.). *Excellent Image Creations,* https://www.frederickhightowerfineart.com/

Huntsville-Madison County Public Library. (2018). *Celebrating African American Culture & History: Home*, https://guides. hmcpl.org/AfricanAmericanHistory

Jacob, J. C. H., & Harrison, J. (2010). *The Art of Elizabeth Catlett: Sculptures and Prints*. Ann Norton Sculpture Gardens, http://elizabethcatlett.net/CATLETT_ANSG.pdf

Justin, R. (2020). *Targeting a statue at A&M and a school song at UT, Texas college students are pushing for a reckoning on race*. The Texas Tribune, https://www.texastribune. org/2020/06/16/sul-ross-am-statue/

Kent, Fred and Nikitin, Cynthia. (2012). *Collaborative, Creative Placemaking: Good Public Art Depends on Good Public Spaces*, https://www.pps.org/article/collaborative-creative-placemaking-good-public-art-depends-on-good-public-spaces

LIB Quotes. (n.d.). *Meta Vaux Warrick Fuller Quotes*, https:// libquotes.com/meta-vaux-warrick-fuller/quote/lba6v7x

Mack, F. (2007). *Selma Hortense Burke* (1900-1995). Black Past, https://www.blackpast.org/african-american-history/ burke-selma-hortense-1900-1995/

Mary Ellen Gallery. (n.d.). *John Wilson*, https:// maryryangallery.com/artists/john-wilson/

McAdams, A. (2020). *Chicago police investigate vandalism at George Washington memorial, Christopher Columbus statue*. ABC Chicago, https://abc7chicago.com/george-washington-statue-defaced-on-south-side/6247424/

Mio, L. (2020). *Oliver LaGrone: Sculptor, Poet, Educator, and Humanitarian*. Cranbrook Kitchen Sink, https:// cranbrookkitchensink.wordpress.com/2020/02/14/ oliver-lagrone-sculptor-poet-educator-and-humanitarian/

Mother of Humanity. (2015). *About the Artist Nijel Binns*, https://motherofhumanity.org/monument/about-the-artist/

National Park Service. (2016). *African Burial Ground: National Monument, New York*, https://www.nps.gov/afbg/learn/historyculture/ancestral-chamber.htm

Nock, G. (n.d.). *George Nock Fine Art*, https://www.georgenock.com/home

Oolite Arts. (n.d.). *Alumni Michael Richards 1997 – 2000*, https://oolitearts.org/resident/michael-richards/

Porter, A. P. (n.d.-a). *the blog from the edge*, https://anthonypeytonporter.com/index.html

Porter, A. P. (n.d.-b). *The Past*, https://anthonypeytonporter.com/blog/about/

Reference.com. (2020). *How Does Art Affect Culture and Society? https*://www.reference.com/world-view/art-influence-society-466abce706f18fd0

Saburi Ayubu, K. (2010). *The Sculpture of Michael Rolando Richards*. Black Art Depot Today, https://blackartblog.blackartdepot.com/features/featured-ethnic-artist/michael-rolando-richards.html

Shea, A. (2020). *16 Statues And Memorials Were Damaged During Sunday's Protests, Including One Dedicated To African American Soldiers*. WBUR, https://www.wbur.org/artery/2020/06/03/16-statues-memorials-damaged

Silvarole, G. (2019). *That Frederick Douglass statue is down again. Here's why*. Democrat & Chronicle, https://www.democratandchronicle.com/story/news/2019/04/11/frederick-

Southern Poverty Law Center. (2019). *Whose Heritage? Public Symbols of the Confederacy*, https://www.splcenter.org/20190201/ whose-heritage-public-symbols-confederacy

Sullivan, V. (n.d.). *Welcome To Vixon Sullivan Art,* https://www.vixonsullivan.com/

Summers, M. (2007). *Richmond Barthé* (1901-1989), https://www.blackpast.org/african-american-history/barthe-richmond-1901-1988/

Sutherland, C. (2007). *Meta Warrick Fuller (1877-1968).* Black Past, https://www.blackpast.org/african-american-history/fuller-meta-warrick-1877-1968/

Taylor, D. (2020). *Birmingham's Charles Linn and his fallen statue.* *WRBL,* https://www.wrbl.com/news/alabama-news/birminghams-charles-linn-and-his-fallen-statue/

The Baltimore Sun. (2007). *James E. Lewis, Morgan State sculptor and champion of black artists,* https://www.baltimoresun.com/features/bal-blackhistory-lewis-story.html

The History Makers. (2005). *Elizabeth Catlett's Biography (1915-2012),* https://www.thehistorymakers.org/biography/elizabeth-catlett-41

The Johnson Collection (n.d). *Barthé, Richmond (1901-1989),* https://thejohnsoncollection.org/richmond-barthe/

The Philanthropy Roundtable. (n.d.) *Oseola McCarty,* https://www.philanthropyroundtable.org/almanac/people/hall-of-fame/detail/oseola-mccarty

The University of North Carolina at Chapel Hill. (2020). *Unsung Founders Memorial: Virtual Black And Blue Tour,* http://blackandblue.web.unc.edu/stops-on-the-tour/unsung-founders/

University of Mississippi. (2006). *University Sets Oct. 1 Dedication for Civil Rights Monument.* Newswise, https://www.newswise.com/

articles/university-sets-oct-1-dedication-for-civil-rights-monument

University Museum at Texas Southern (n.d). *The Carroll Harris Simms Collection,* https://www.umusetsu.org/the-carroll-har

Wardlaw, A. (n.d.). *Simms, Carroll H.* Texas State Historical Association, https://www.tshaonline.org/handbook/entries/simms-carroll-harris

Warikoo, N. (2020). *Statue of former Dearborn Mayor Orville Hubbard taken down.* Detroit Free Press, https://www.freep.com/story/news/local/michigan/wayne/2020/06/05/statue-dearborn-mayor-orville-hubbard-removed/3161044001/

CPSIA information can be obtained
at www.ICGtesting.com
Printed in the USA
LVHW011350031120
670577LV00005B/484